Chapter 7 Snack Recipes 77

Chapter 8 Dessert Recipes...86

Chapter 1: Introduction of Renal Diet

How does your Kidney Function?

When you know you have a kidney problem, be it a minor kidney dysfunction, or a kidney failure or something as serious as kidney dialysis or even severe kidney damage, to take care of your kidney health first you need to know, how does the kidney function? Every organ of our body has a purpose, and the primary purpose of a kidney is to remove waste from your body. The kidney actually gets rid of the extra potassium, sodium, phosphorous and fluids. When someone suffers from renal diseases, the kidney does not function as actively as a healthy person. This is the reason why a renal diet encourages to limit the consumption of these nutrients.

When you put so much of these nutrients, the kidney gets pressurized, and it is advised by doctors to give your kidney rest as much as possible by decreasing the intake of sodium, potassium, phosphate, and protein.

You cannot leave protein all together from the diet because you may face sudden weight loss which is not suitable for the overall health. Protein also develops muscle mass, so a healthy dosage of protein is essential every single day.
When you add too much sodium in your food, your kidney gets severely pressurized. Kidney patients should consume potassium and phosphate too but within limits. Coping with the new eating habit would take time, but you need to think about the larger picture and the health of your kidney. A damaged kidney can still survive with some precautions.

What Renal Failure Can Cause?

There are more risk factors to atherosclerosis than the traditional explanation of the risk factors. 10.6% of people suffer from genetic variants for CHD. 40% of people face the residual risk factor of cardiovascular events.

LDL-C cannot predict the changes of atherosclerosis. Resistant atherosclerosis means having carotid plaque issues even though they have a low level of LDL-C. In a stroke preventive clinic had half of its patients who have resistant atherosclerosis. It is a hypothesis that renal function triggers resistant atherosclerosis.

To prevent cardiovascular mortality, renal failure has to stop. Renal failure triggers cardiovascular mortality. People suffering from CKD-Chronic Kidney Disease have a higher chance of cardiovascular disease. Due to renal failure, people have decreased life expectancy.

Uremic toxins like asymmetric dimethylarginine, homocysteine (tHcy), thiocyanate and a nitric oxide antagonist, triggers renal failure. The kidney excretes intestinal microbiome which may get residual effects in renal function. Elderly patients have eGFR- estimated glomerular filtration rate 60, which makes them high risked patients of cardiovascular disease. This is why many people go on a vegetarian diet.

The Stroke Prevention Clinic ran research that studies how renal impairment can cause coronary diseases. The study was supported by blood sampling, the intestinal microbiome was studied, and Trimethylamine n-oxide was also studied. Reserved phase Chromatography was used.

Even they studied how much food consumption took place in the previous year. The cholesterol level, TMAO level was also measured.

The Role of Sodium in our Body

A renal patient has to cut down on sodium and potassium on a daily basis in order to keep their kidney at rest. Before you limit your sodium and potassium intake, you should know what role they play in our body. Sodium and salt are not interchangeable. People have the misconception that the only salt contains sodium, but there are natural foods that are high on sodium too. Salt is a mixture of chloride and sodium. Canned food and processed food have a large amount of sodium in them. A renal patient has to consider that fact that natural food can contain sodium too.

Our body has three significant electrolytes, sodium, potassium and chloride. Sodium regulates blood vessels and blood pressure, regulates muscle contraction, nerve function, regulates the acid balance in the blood, and keep the balance of fluid in the body! The kidney usually excretes the toxin in our body, but a damaged kidney cannot get rid of the extra sodium in our body. So when a renal patient consumes too much sodium, it gets stored in the blood vessels and bloodstream. This storage of sodium can lead to feeling thirsty all the time. This is a bit problematic as a kidney patient has to limit their fluid intake. It can cause edema, high blood pressure, breathless, and even heart failure. So a renal patient must always limit their sodium intake. The average limit is 150 mg per snacks and 400 mg per meal.

The Role of Potassium in Our Body

Potassium maintains the balance of electrolyte and fluid in our bloodstream. It also regulates our heartbeat and contributes to our muscle function. Potassium can be found in many fruits, vegetables, and meat; it also exists in our own body. A healthy kidney keeps the required potassium in our body and removes the excess through urine.

A damaged kidney is not capable of removing potassium anymore. Therefore is it essential for a renal patient to watch how much potassium they are consuming. Hyperkalemia is a condition when you have too much potassium in the blood. Hyperkalemia can cause slow pulse, weak muscles, irregular heart rate, heart attack, and even death.

To control your potassium intake on a daily basis, count every ingredient's potassium level. A renal expert dietitian would be helpful to consult as they know which ingredient would work best for your condition. There are seasonings available in the super-shops which are high in potassium, avoid these items. Food like avocado, beans, spinach, fish, bananas, and potatoes are very high in potassium. Even if you are eating these ingredients, try to divide the serving in half and eat a small serving. Do not eat these high potassium ingredients every single day. There are much low potassium foods available, pick them when you are making your meal plan. Fresh ingredients are always better than the frozen kind. To keep track of your potassium intake throughout the day, keep a personal food journal where you can input everything and reflect when you need to.

The Role of Phosphorous in Our Body

Phosphorous contribute to keep our bone strong and develop it. Phosphorous helps in muscle movement, develops the connective tissue and organs. While we eat food that contains phosphorous, the small intestines store it to develop our bones. A well-functioning kidney can get rid of the extra phosphorous in the body, but a damaged one cannot do so. So renal patients have to watch how much phosphorous they are consuming.

As phosphorous helps to develop bones, it can also weaken the bones by extracting calcium from it if too much phosphorous is consumed. The calcium removed from the bones gets deposited to blood vessels, heart, eyes, and lungs which can cause severe health problems.

To keep the balance of phosphorous for a renal patient, the proper knowledge of high phosphorous food is required. Red meat is very high in phosphorous. Milk is very high in phosphorous. Fast food like burgers, pizzas, fries is high in phosphorous. Fizzy drinks that are colored are high in phosphorous. Canned fish and seeds are quite high in phosphorous.

Packaged food or canned food is often high in phosphorous. Read the labels before you purchase any canned goods from the supermarket. Phosphorous binders are excellent way to keep your phosphorous intake to a minimum. If you ask you your dietitian, they will give you an excellent phosphorous binder, which you can follow to keep track of how much you can and should consume.

Nutrients you should avoid when you have a kidney disease

When you have kidney problems, you must count your calories and carefully consume any nutrition. There are a few things you must do to prevent kidney related problems. Renal diet contributes to making your kidney health better and omits and includes everything that is required.

Sodium is absolutely prohibited in the renal diet because it damages the kidney. When you are seasoning your food, be sure to use other herbs and spices than salt. While grocery shopping, do not buy anything that has added salt in it. Some of the canned food is pre-seasoned, try to avoid them as they contain salt in it.

Potassium builds muscle work, and it can cause kidney damage when consumed at a higher rate. Avoid food that is high in potassium like, banana, cantaloupe, dried beans, squash, pumpkin, green leafy vegetables like collard, lettuce, kale, etc. Molasses, granola, cereal, sweet potatoes, and potatoes are high in potassium too. Phosphorus can also contribute to making your kidney disease worse. Dairy has a lot of Phosphorus, so you need to limit your dairy intake. Mushrooms, Brussels sprouts, broccoli should be eaten in moderation too. You can enjoy 1 cup of milk a day. You can eat one serving of granola per week. If you eat bread, go for white bread than grain bread.

Soft drinks and beer contain a high amount of Phosphorus. So limit your beverages or try to avoid them altogether if possible. If you must drink soft drinks, try to drink only the clear ones.

Adapting to a new lifestyle to minimize your kidney problems

Patients who are suffering from kidney failure, going through kidney dialysis and have renal impairments need to not only go through medical treatment but also change their eating habit, lifestyle to make the situation better. Many researches have been done on this, and the conclusion is food has a lot to do with how your kidney functions and its overall health.

The first thing to changing your lifestyle is knowing about how your kidney functions and how different food can trigger different reactions in the kidney function. There are certain nutrients that affect your kidney directly. Nutrients like sodium, protein, phosphate, and potassium are the risky ones. You do not have to omit them altogether from your diet, but you need to limit or minimize their intake as much as possible. You cannot leave out essential nutrient like protein from your diet, but you need to count how much protein you are having per day. This is essential in order to keep balance in your muscles and maintaining a good functioning kidney.

A vast change in kidney patients is measuring how much fluid they are drinking. This is a crucial change in every kidney patient, and you must adapt to this new eating habit. Too much water or any other form of liquid can disrupt your kidney function. How much fluid you can consume depends on the condition of your kidney. Most people assign separate bottles for them so that they can measure how much they have drunk and how much more they can drink throughout the day.

Chapter 2: Everything You Need to Know About Renal Diet

Things you should know before Starting a Renal diet

If you have kidney failure, damaged kidney or symptoms of kidney problems then you must follow a renal diet. The renal diet focuses more on the foods you should avoid because they are directly detrimental to your kidney health.

Renal diet controls your consumption of sodium, protein, potassium and phosphorous. A renal diet contributes to preventing renal failure.

Below are a list of food/nutrients you should avoid preventing kidney related problems.

Protein: Being on a renal diet, you should intake 0.75 kg protein per day. Good source of protein are eggs, milk, cheese, meat, nuts, and fish.

Sodium: Adding salt is very important in our food, but when you are suffering from kidney problems, you have to omit or minimize your salt intake. Too much sodium intake can trigger high blood pressure and fluid retention in the body. You need to find substitutes that help season your food. Herbs and spices that are extracted from plants are a good option. Using garlic, pepper, mustard can increase the taste of your food without adding any salt. Avoid artificial "salts" that are low in sodium because they are high in potassium, which is also dangerous for kidney health.

Potassium: After getting diagnosed, if your results show your potassium level is high in the blood, then you should restrict your potassium intake. Baked and fried potatoes are very high in potassium. Leafy greens, fruit juices are high in potassium. You can still enjoy vegetables that are low in potassium.

Phosphate: Consumption of phosphate becomes dangerous when kidney failure reaches 80% and goes to the 4th/5th stage of kidney failure. So it is best to be safe than sorry. Minimize your phosphate intake by counting the calories and minerals.

How Food can Impact on improving your Chronic Kidney Disease

When you are suffering from chronic kidney disease, along with your medical treatment, you also need to make a few changes to your eating habit too. The type of food, the type of nutrient you are consuming on a daily basis impacts on your kidney health, and it can actually improve or decrease your kidney function.

The changes that you need to get used to are limiting or restricting your sodium intake, endorsing a low protein diet, do not drink too much fluid, limiting or restricting your phosphate, potassium and other electrolytes.

Sometimes people who are suffering from chronic kidney disease face sudden weight loss; in that case, you need to increase your calorie intake so your weight can get to a healthy range.   When you are doing kidney dialysis, you need to alter your food habits more often. You need to be monitoring your health condition and kidney's condition every month to check if the diet you are on is working for you or not.

A diet helps to prevent unnecessary food and nutrient intake when your body can work better with a little limitation on certain nutrients. If you limit or count the minerals, fluid, and electrolytes on a daily basis, you would see positive changes in your kidney health.

Especially the patients who are facing kidney dialysis should avoid building up waste products in the body. When you eat carefully, you can avoid the buildup of waste materials in your body. The most important thing a kidney patient must do is limit their fluid intake per day.

Managing Your Renal Diet When You are a Diabetic

A diabetic patient has to control their food choices on a daily basis when you start a renal diet while you have diabetes, things can get stricter. Even if it becomes strict, it needs to be done in order to keep your kidney functioning and keep the blood sugar level under control at the same time.

To cater to a diabetic renal patient, a customized meal plan has to be made. We have talked about monitoring the progress of a renal patient; it is even crucial to monitor a diabetic renal patient's progress. Without a certified diabetic educator and a dietitian, it is not possible to make a customized meal plan.

Unless you are overweight, a renal patient does not have to count the carbohydrate, but a diabetic renal patient has to limit their carbohydrate intake. You need to balance potassium, sodium, protein, carbohydrate, and phosphate. A lot of healthy choices have to be made. A wise decision about food and meal plan can make the journey much easier.

After going through your meal plan for a week, check your blood sugar level. If it is normal, then continue the same meal plan for another two weeks. Again go for a blood test to check your blood sugar level. You need to regularly check your blood sugar level because when it raises or goes down, other health problems start occurring. Diabetic patients usually suffer from obesity, so try to have healthy body weight. Do not get overwhelmed or stressed as it would affect your health severely.

Food That Can Be Eaten in the Renal Diet

The renal diet focuses on more on what not to eat to improve your kidney health. But it is also essential to know what would actually benefit a kidney patient or someone who has renal dysfunction. There should be clarity regarding how much minerals, nutrients, and fluids one can eat during a renal diet.

We know renal diet endorses to limit your protein intake, but does this mean it is not essential to eat protein on a renal diet? No, you should definitely eat about 7-8 ounces of protein every single day. You should have one meal dedicated to protein which would contain 7-8 ounce. It is essential to combat infections. It also balances muscle mass. This is a healthy way to limit your protein intake on a renal diet. The sources of protein are many, milk, egg, meat, fish, pulses, etc. There are other plant-based proteins too like soy, mushroom, etc.

You should eat fresh vegetables and fruits which would be low in sodium and fat. They should not be frozen, because in most cases, frozen ingredients have preservatives in them. Some of the frozen foods also contain seasonings too. When you are picking your vegetables, make sure to stay far away from the ones that have a large quantity of potassium. When you sit and list your ingredients, you would find more things are on the positive list than the omitted ingredients list. So enjoy the food, enjoy the process of this diet to live a better life.

Ways to Stay on a Renal Diet

A renal diet is designed for patients who are suffering from kidney damage, kidney dialysis, and dysfunctional kidney. The diet helps to put your kidney at rest and balances the pH level of the blood. Food consumption has a vital role in keeping your kidney healthy and functioning.

The very first step is to limit your sodium, potassium, phosphate and protein intake. Of course, it is much easier said than done! But there are few tips that if tried, your renal diet journey can become less stressful.

When preparing your food, keep it less salty. The ingredients that you are using check their labels. Checking labels help you determine how much sodium you are consuming per day. There are many ingredients that have hidden sodium in it.

Ingredients like baking powder, dressings, and processed powdered soup have hidden sodium in it.

Choosing fresh ingredients is always beneficial for renal patients. Eating seasonal food is an excellent way to find fresh vegetables and fruits. If you have to choose frozen food, go for the un-salty and unflavored kind. Canned food comes in high potassium and high sodium liquid. Choose the ones that are clear.

When you do go out to eat, choose renal friendly dishes. Order the drinks that are low sodium and low potassium. Clear ones are better than the colored ones. Choose healthy protein options. Divide your fluid into four different portions and drink them after certain hours to keep your thirst satisfied and without hurting the renal fluid limits.

Dishes a Dialysis Patient Can Order at Restaurants

A renal patient while going through dialysis has to be very careful about what they eat or drink. But does it mean you cannot enjoy dining out? Certainly not, you can enjoy eating at restaurants, but you need to be careful about what you are ordering. There are many people who take the menu of their favorite restaurants and show it to their dietitian and the dietitian mark which dishes are safe for a dialysis patient to eat.

Usually, the dishes in any restaurants are quite high in sodium and potassium, sometime in phosphate too, while ordering you need to ask them if they can cater to your condition and make you a unique dish that is low on protein, potassium, sodium, and phosphate. Ask them to give you a dish made from fresh ingredients rather than canned ones.

Italian and Asian food are safer options than others as they have a little seasoning and there are no greasy sauces. Even if they come with sauces, ask them not to pour the sauce on your food, instead pour it on the side or in a separate bowl.

If you go to a Chinese restaurant, you can order steamed rice, egg rolls, stir fry vegetables, dim sum, etc. In Thai restaurant, beef, chicken skewers, spring roll, pad thai noodles, grilled chicken/fish, etc. In Japanese restaurants, you can order sashimi, tempura, etc. In Italian restaurants, you can order pasta without the sauce or sauce on the side. Try to skip soups because they have a lot of flavorings.

Smart Snacking Options for Renal Patients

It is absolutely human to crave for snacks no matter what situation you are in. Even when someone is sick, they still crave for snacks. Renal patients have to stay under a renal diet 24/7 to prevent unwanted renal failure. So, how to give in to your cravings whilst being on a renal diet? This solution is simple, you need to choose a snack that is in sync with your renal diet, and that does not make your situation worse.

There are many healthy snacking options for renal patients. Your snacks have to be adequately counted where they would not cross the limit of sodium, potassium, phosphate and protein intake per day. A good renal snack should be less than 80mg phosphorous, less than 130 mg potassium.

Some patients can enjoy more than other patients, to find out how much nutrients you can consume daily, you need to check with your doctor or dietitian.

One cup of Popcorn, rice cereal, pretzels, blueberries (fresh), 2 breadsticks, ½ of a muffin, ½ of bagel, ½ cup sorbet, fruit cocktail are few healthy snacking ideas. 2 Fig cookies, ½ cup oats, one apple, few grapes (10-15pieces), vanilla wafers, etc. can also be enjoyed. You should not go for snacks 5-6 times a day. Instead build a healthy snacking cycle where you only crave for it when you are actually hungry. Do not give into your snacking craving every single time you have an urge for it.

Eat as a Renal Patient for One Day!

If you are someone who has recently been diagnosed with kidney problems, then reading this article would help as it would give you a glimpse of how a renal patient eat on a daily basis.

A renal patient limits their sodium, phosphorous, protein and potassium intake. So usually no salt is better but if you are adding salt, keep it very minimum. Do not use any salt substitute as they are low in sodium but high in potassium.

2-3 serving (3 ounces per serving) of protein is essential every day. Lean protein like fish, white meat, milk, and eggs are a good option. A small portion of natural cheese can be added to the meal. Need to make sure you do not cross 8 ounces protein limit though.

If you want dessert, you can have a ½ serving of ice cream, sorbet, yogurt or milk. Need to omit nuts, seeds, and legumes as they are high in potassium.

Pick fresh fruits to eat. If it is a medium sized fruit, you can have one fruit per day. If they are small berries, you can have half a cup a day. They should be low potassium fruits.

You can have two servings of vegetables per day. If they are cooked, you can have ½ cup per serving, and if they are raw, you can have 1 cup per serving.

Honey, syrups, oil, butter, and mayo can be used to enhance the taste of the food.

Need to limit the fluid intake to 4-6 cups per day. If you are a dialysis patient, it needs to be no less than 4 cups.

Chapter 3: Tips and FAQs

Tips on Controlling Your Phosphorous

Being on a renal diet, you must control how much phosphorous you are consuming daily. Patients suffering from renal failure need to control their phosphorous intake, but they cannot omit it all together from the diet because this nutrition is also essential for the body to be healthy. A person with a healthy kidney has no trouble in getting rid of the excess phosphorous, but a renal patient cannot get rid of the excess phosphorous efficiently. When excess phosphorus builds up in the blood, it triggers problems like muscle aches, broken bones, inactivity of the joints, heart and blood vessels.

Start by omitting or limiting very high phosphorous food such as red meat, dairy, fish, and eggs. Cheese is also very high in phosphorous, if you have it, try to limit between 4 ounces.

Beans of any kind are very high in phosphorous. Dried vegetables and fruits have a higher level of phosphorous than fresh ones. So pick fresh ingredients all the time. Unrefined grains are high in phosphorous, choose white grains. Colored sodas are very high in phosphorous, while picking sodas, choose the clear ones.

Every patient is different so you may face different phosphorous limit based on the condition of your kidney and body. So it is essential to be under treatment and check your phosphorous level. Bind yourself to the limit your doctor sets while you are prepping your meals or eating outside. Try not to exceed it. Most doctors give s 1000 mg limit for phosphorous intake.

Tips on Controlling Your Fluid Intake

Patients with kidney failure or renal failure must control how much fluid they are drinking per day. For an average person, the limit is eight glasses or 2 liters to stay healthy. For a renal patient is 4 cups of fluid per day. When a renal patient is on kidney dialysis, they have to be even more careful because urination puts pressure on their lungs and heart. Without water or tea, a renal patient can have 500 ml of fluid. This means your meals can contain 500 ml of fluid and you can drink 4 cups of water per day.

If you are newly diagnosed with renal disease, then you would need some time to adapt to the new lifestyle, but you need to account the fact that it is for the betterment of your health. You need to adjust here and there and make sure you are not crossing the fluid limit on any given cause.

Always keep your bottle separate where you can count how much water you are drinking. Try to divide the portion for different hours. For example, for the morning time, keep one cup of water, for the lunch hour, keep one cup of water, etc. When you have popsicles or fruit ices, count them as fluid as well because they will melt as soon as you eat them.

While prepping for meals, count how much fluid your meals have. It should not exceed over 500 ml per day.

Tips on Controlling Your Protein Intake

When you have renal disease, you must control your protein intake. You cannot omit protein all together from your diet because it is essential for muscle mass. Protein also helps to combat infections in the body, heals any scar faster, so if you lake sufficient protein in the body, your immune system will get damaged. Protein is also essential to maintain body tissue, and it provides energy to the body. So a renal patient should take protein daily but not more than 7 to 8 ounces daily.

There are many protein options like veal, beef, turkey, chicken, duck, egg, fish and seafood. If you think 8 ounces per meal is not sufficient enough to give you energy then add some sides like vegetable stir fry or a white bread slice. You can also pair your protein in shakes. But if you have shakes, make sure to count that fluid too.

If you are someone who does not enjoy eating non-vegetarian food, there are many plant-based proteins too. Mushroom, soy, lentils, avocado, are good to provide protein to your body. If you do not want to have 8 ounces of protein in one meal, then you can also divide them into 2 or 3 different meals. You can also divide it into your snacks as well. One egg is equivalent to 1 ounce of protein, so starting your day with an egg for breakfast is a good idea. At the end of the day, you should have about 8 ounces of protein every day to have a healthy body.

How do Kidney Patients Eat Outside?

A kidney patient has to maintain a balanced diet every single day. It is not like your regular diet where there are cheat days, and you can enjoy food as you please! You can enjoy food, but you have to always balance your menu. How much nutrient and fluid you are consuming is very important to count. Food has a lot to do with how well your kidney would function. A damaged kidney still can survive for a long time if the diet is maintained properly and carefully.

It would take some effort, and you would have to be determined to maintain a balanced diet. A renal diet is suitable for kidney patients in any condition. It explains how sodium can make you thirsty and increases your desire to drink more fluid. It explains too much potassium, phosphate and protein can damage the kidney sooner. Being on a renal diet, you can manage to eat properly at home, but the big question is how do you survive when you eat at the restaurants occasionally? The procedure is not as complicated as you may think. Whenever you are eating outside, pick something that is in sync with renal diet. The renal diet limits the sodium intake, so when ordering food, ask for less seasoning in your food. When you are ordering drinks, make sure to order clear drinks with no artificial flavoring. Avoid ingredients that are too high on potassium and phosphate. If you are ordering any protein, make sure it is not more than 8 ounce per serving.

Can Renal Patients enjoy Fast Food?

Fast food is something that is a favorite for everyone, and no matter what the dietitian or doctors say, the craving for fast food does not get diminished. So when a renal patient craves for fast food, how to deal with it? You need to order carefully and do not add anything to your menu that does not match your renal diet criteria. If you want to order burgers and sandwiches that are premade, they are most likely very salty, so you need to ask if they can make you a new one with limited salt. Fries are perhaps the most ordered fast food ever, but they are very salty, and potato is high in potassium. If you must eat it, ask for no salt and order a tiny amount. When you are ordering anything, ask them to add the sauces on the side or in a different bowl. The sauces are usually very high in sodium. If they provide you a different bowl or they spread the sauce on the side, you can control how much of it you are going to eat.

When you are eating at a food court, consider other food options that you can pair with your fast food. Count the nutrients you are consuming. Never cross the limits. Fast food joints usually serve deep fried food the most, but they also have shallowly fried and baked items as well. Try to choose the baked ones over the deep fried ones. Avoid ordering extra crispy items as they are saltier.

What would a Renal Patient Eat During Holidays?

During the festive season, it is mostly about getting together with friends and family and eating your favorite meals. Holiday food is extravagant, delicious and powerhouse of protein, sodium, and potassium. A renal patient needs to keep their dietary limit in mind while they dine during holidays. If you take a few extra steps, you do not have to cook separately for a renal patient; they can eat the same food. You need to design your menu in such a way that everyone still can enjoy the food, and the renal diet does not get compromised either.

For appetizers, you can make unsalted popcorn, pretzels, breadsticks, crackers, chicken wings, deviled eggs, vegetable chips, and meatballs, etc. For the main course, you can choose calamari, chicken, beef, turkey, fish, goat, veal, lamb, shrimp, or lamb. You need to make it less salty and if you are making a sauce, keep it in a separate bowl. You can add vegetables to your primary course as well or use vegetables to make side dishes too. Vegetables that are good for renal patients are green beans, cabbage, eggplant, corn, carrots, zucchini, cauliflower, broccoli, okra, spaghetti squash, etc. A lot of these vegetables are used in holiday cooking anyway, so you do not have to do anything extra. While cooking these vegetables, try to keep the salt to a minimum so your renal patient can enjoy just like others. For beverages, make something that is clear, has no artificial flavoring or chemicals.

Should I meet a Dietitian while I am in a Renal Diet?

Renal patients invariably follow a strict diet where they limit their sodium, potassium, protein and phosphate intake. They need to do it in order to stop damaging their kidney further and keep them active. Renal diet often talks about the food or nutrient renal patients should avoid, but it hardly focuses on the type of food or dishes renal patients should eat. Many patients who are new to this diet get confused and cannot make a proper meal plan. Renal patients know they have to cut back on sodium, potassium, phosphate, and protein but in what proportion they should consume these nutrients is a mystery to many. To clear the mystery, a renal patient must consult a dietitian who can make two weeks of meal plan for them. If you continue the diet for two weeks, you would have a proper idea about how the meal plan works, and you would be able to make your own meal plan for the other time.

Kidney damage has different stages as well. What is valid for a patient in stage 1 to eat may not be valid for a patient who is on stage 3 or stage 4. This is very relevant, and it is, in fact, essential to know in which stage you are on and eat accordingly. The fluid intake, the protein intake also would vary from person to person. You cannot take a sheet that has the average limit of nutrient for a kidney patient and thinks it is ideal for you too. You need to get diagnosed and then find out what is right for you.

Does Following an Alkaline Diet Helps Renal Patients?

A kidney is one of the most critical organs in our body as it balances the fluid in our body and gets rid of the toxic elements. A kidney filters out 180 liters of blood on a daily basis. So, whether you are a renal patient or not, you should take extra care for this organ. The pH level of blood is a core element to a healthy kidney. The food you consume can balance the pH level of the blood. A good functioning kidney has a pH level of blood is 7.35-7.45pH. A renal patient obviously fell behind here. The alkaline or acid when eliminates to a drastic degree, even death can follow. To avoid chronic illness, like obesity, kidney stones, diabetes, gas, joint pain, headaches, and kidney diseases alkaline forming food come to rescue.

This is the purpose of the alkaline diet and renal diet by nature is a lot like alkaline diet anyway. Some even consider the alkaline diet as the best kidney diet out there. The food that you consume in an alkaline diet balances your pH levels and gives your kidney rest. The kidney does not have to go through the extra work. The idea is to create alkaline/acid in the blood, but do not gallop acidic food to create it. The alkaline diet focuses on unprocessed food and fresh ingredients. It avoids red meat and dairy. So your kidney can rest, and the pH level of the blood is still restored.

How Important is Monitoring your Progress in Renal Diet?

Kidney patients are not your average dieters; they need to check the renal diet they are doing is helping them or not benefitting them! The kidney is a vital organ, and without a well-functioning kidney, your entire body collapses. So when you are on a renal diet, after passing two weeks, you should immediately check with your health caregiver or your dietitian to see if the diet is working for your benefit. The monitor has to be done by you; you need to keep a journal of the things you are eating and drinking and in what portion. What works for an average kidney patient may not work for you. Your pH level of blood, your kidney stage, and your weight and age would determine what serving size is right for you. The fluid capacity of a patient can also vary depending on the kidney's condition. A patient who is under dialysis would have to eat and drink differently than an average renal patient.

So monitoring and consulting your doctor or dietitian is very important. Sometimes the renal patients face severe weight loss due to the new eating habits. In that case, the dietitian would increase the protein and carbohydrate in the meal plans. Everything has to be balanced. Anything excess or anything less is not acceptable in the renal diet! You need to hit the exact benchmark where the limit lies in terms of nutrition. If you consume more than you should, your kidney would have to filter more, and it would not be able to rest. If you eat less than you should, your body can collapse and lead to more severe problems.

Why Paying Attention to Serving Size is Essential?

When you are on a renal diet, you have to be careful of what you eat, and in what sizes you are eating it. This is not your average diet, you have a special kidney condition, and with little effort on food, you can actually live a healthier life. Medical treatment is essential while you have renal disease, but food can minimize your renal problems and avoid visiting the hospitals more often.

The renal diet focuses on consuming food that is low in sodium, potassium, phosphate, and protein and high in carbohydrate. The fluid intake has to be limited too. Serving size of any ingredient or dish is essential because you are on a limited nutrient range where if you go higher than your range or lower than your range, it can trigger unnecessary illness. Your kidney function may get disrupted due to eating a little more sodium than your limit. Taking note of the serving size of food is very important when you are going grocery shopping when you are eating outside at a restaurant. When you are preparing meals at home, you should count the nutrition and then prepare the food. Read the labels properly; every ingredient that you buy should have a proper nutrition value explained. A slight overboard on the nutrition level can lead to damaging your kidney further. You need to give your kidney rest and to do it all you need to do is follow the renal diet properly. Stay within your nutrient limit on a daily basis.

Chapter 4 Breakfast Recipes

Breakfast Oatmeal Muffins with Berries

Serves: 12
Cooking Time: 22 minutes

Ingredients:
1 cup unbleached all-purpose flour
2 eggs
1 orange, the grated zest only
1 lemon, the grated zest
1 tbsp lemon juice
1/2 cup quick-cooking oatmeal
1/2 tsp baking soda
1/2 cup applesauce
1/4 cup canola oil
2/3 cup lightly packed brown sugar
3/4 cup raspberries, fresh or frozen
3/4 cup blueberries, fresh or frozen

Directions for Cooking:
1) With the rack in the middle position, preheat the oven to 350°F. Line 12 muffin cups with paper liners.
2) In a bowl, combine the flour, oatmeal, brown sugar, and baking soda. Set aside.
3) In a large bowl, whisk the eggs, applesauce, oil, citrus zest and lemon juice. With a wooden spoon, stir in the dry ingredients. Add the berries and stir gently.
4) Scoop into the muffin cups. Bake for 20 to 22 minutes or until a toothpick inserted in the center of a muffin comes out clean.
5) Let cool. Store muffins in airtight containers and will last for a week.

Nutrition Information:
Calories per Serving: 191; carbs: 31g; protein: 4g; fats: 7g; phosphorus: 56mg; potassium: 106mg; sodium: 37mg

Blueberry-Oat Pancakes

Serves: 10
Cooking Time: 60 minutes

Ingredients:
½ cup + 2 tbsps agave nectar
1 cup frozen blueberries
½ cup Greek yogurt, vanilla flavor
1 cup milk
1 egg
½ tsp baking soda
½ tsp baking powder
1 cup whole wheat flour
1/8 tsp sea salt
½ cup steel cut oats
1 ½ cups water

Directions for Cooking:
1) On high fire, place a medium pot, add water and bring to a boil.
2) Once boiling add salt and oats. Lower fire to a simmer and cook for ten minutes or until oats are tender.
3) Turn off fire and set aside.
4) Whisk egg in a medium bowl. Add yogurt and milk and whisk well.
5) Sift in baking soda, baking powder and whole wheat pastry flour. Whisk well to combine.
6) Fold in cooked oats and blueberries.
7) On medium fire, place a nonstick fry pan and grease with cooking spray.
8) Pour ¼ cup of the batter into fry pan and cook for 2-3 minutes or until pancake is bubbly. Turnover pancake and cook for a minute. Remove pancake and place in a serving plate.
9) Repeat process for remaining batter until done.
10) Serve and enjoy with your favorite syrup.

Nutrition Information:
Calories per Serving: 94; carbs: 16g; protein: 5g; fats: 3g; phosphorus: 144mg; potassium: 165mg; sodium: 119mg

Slow Cooked Breakfast Oatmeal

Serves: 8
Cooking Time: 8 hours

Ingredients:
1 tsp cinnamon
1 tsp molasses
1/3 cup dried apricots, chopped
1/3 cup dried cherries
1/3 cup raisins
2 cups steel-cut oats
4 cups water
4 cups fat-free milk

Directions for Cooking:
1) Place all ingredients in a slow cooker.
2) On low settings, cook oatmeal while covered for 8 to 9 hours.
3) When done, equally transfer into bowls, serve and enjoy.
4)

Nutrition Information:
Calories per Serving: 121; carbs: 27g; protein: 9g; fats: 2g; phosphorus: 303mg; potassium: 425mg; sodium: 69mg

Breakfast Banana Delight

Serves: 4
Cooking Time: minutes

Ingredients:
½ tsp nutmeg
1 cup banana (chopped)
1 tbsp oil
¼ cup egg substitute
½ cup skim milk
1 tbsp sodium free baking powder
1 tbsp sugar
1 cup flour

Directions for Cooking:
1) In a bowl, mix and stir baking powder, sugar and flour.

2) In a separate bowl, combine oil, egg and milk then add nutmeg and banana.

3) Add the mixture into the bowl of dry ingredients.

4) In a hot frying pan, drop just by tablespoonfuls and fry for about 2 to 3 minutes.

5) Wait until it is golden brown then drain and serve.

Nutrition Information:
Calories per Serving: 270; carbs: 55g; protein: 7g; fats: 5g; phosphorus: 350mg; potassium: 350mg; sodium: 48mg

Cereal with Cranberry-Orange Twist

Serves: 1
Cooking Time: 5 minutes

Ingredients:
1/4 cup dried cranberries
1/3 cup oat bran
½ cup orange juice
½ cup water

Directions for Cooking:
1) In a bowl, combine all ingredients.
2) For about 2 minutes, microwave the bowl then serve with sugar and milk. You may also add honey.
3) Enjoy!

Nutrition Information:
Calories per Serving: 171; carbs: 44g; protein: 7g; fats: 3g; phosphorus: 249mg; potassium: 406mg; sodium: 7mg

Sandwich with Spinach and Tuna Salad

Serves: 4
Cooking Time: minutes

Ingredients:
1 cup fresh baby spinach
8 slices 100% whole wheat sandwich bread
¼ tsp freshly ground black pepper
½ tsp salt free seasoning blend
Juice of one lemon
2 tbsps olive oil
½ tsp dill weed
2 ribs celery, diced

Directions for Cooking:
1) In a medium bowl, mix well dill weed, celery, onion, cucumber and tuna.
2) Add lemon juice and olive oil and mix thoroughly.
3) Season with pepper and salt-free seasoning blend.
4) To assemble sandwich, you can toast bread slices, on top of one bread slice layer ½ cup tuna salad, top with ¼ cup spinach and cover with another slice of bread.
5) Repeat procedure to remaining ingredients, serve and enjoy.

Nutrition Information:
Calories per Serving: 320; carbs: 49g; protein: 9g; fats: 12g; phosphorus: 177mg; potassium: 347mg; sodium: 615mg

Herbed and Spiced Grilled Eggplant

Serves: 4
Cooking Time: 40 minutes

Ingredients:
1 tbsp chopped fresh cilantro
¼ tsp freshly ground black pepper
¼ tsp salt
1 tsp red wine vinegar
1 garlic clove, minced
1 tbsp light molasses
2 cups cherry tomatoes, halved
½ yellow onion, finely chopped
1 tbsp olive oil
Pinch of ground cloves
Pinch of ground nutmeg
Pinch of ground ginger
½ tsp curry powder
½ tsp ground coriander
½ tsp ground cumin
1 tsp mustard seed
1 large aubergine eggplant, around 1 ½ lbs.

Directions for Cooking:
1) Grease grill grate with cooking spray and preheat grill to high heat.
2) Trim eggplant and slice in ¼-inch think lengthwise strips.
3) Grill strips of eggplant for 5 minutes per side or until browned and tender.
4) Remove eggplants from fire and keep warm.
5) In a small bowl, mix cloves, nutmeg, ginger, curry, coriander, cumin and mustard seed.
6) On medium high fire, place a medium nonstick skillet and heat oil.
7) Sauté spice mixture for 30 seconds and add onions.
8) Sauté onions for 4 minutes or until soft and translucent.
9) Add vinegar, garlic, molasses and tomatoes. Sauté for 4 minutes or until thickened.
10) Season with pepper and salt. Turn off fire.
11) On four plates, evenly divide grilled eggplant.

12) Evenly top each plate of eggplant with herbed and spiced sauce.
13) Serve and enjoy while warm.

Nutrition Information:
Calories per Serving: 137; carbs: 23g; protein: 3g; fats: 6g; phosphorus: 52mg; potassium: 484mg; sodium: 160mg

Baked Oatmeal with Apple Spice Flavor

Serves: 6
Cooking Time: 40 minutes

Ingredients:
2 tbsps chopped nuts
2 tbsps brown sugar
1 tsp cinnamon
¼ tsp salt
2 cups rolled oats
1 apple, chopped
2 tbsps oil
1 tsp vanilla
1 ½ cups non-fat milk
½ cup applesauce, sweetened
1 egg, beaten

Directions for Cooking:
1) With cooking spray, grease an 8 x 8-inch baking pan and preheat oven to 375oF.
2) In a large bowl, mix oil, vanilla, milk, applesauce and egg. Thoroughly mix.
3) In a medium bowl, combine cinnamon, salt, baking powder and rolled oats.
4) Pour the dry ingredients into the bowl of wet ingredients and mix well.
5) Transfer batter into prepped pan and spread evenly.
6) Pop into the oven and bake for 25 minutes.
7) Remove from oven and sprinkle with nuts and brown sugar.
8) Return to oven and broil for 3 to 4 minutes or until top of oats be bubbly.
9) Remove from oven; let it cool before slicing into 9 equal squares.
10) You can serve right away or store in tightly lidded containers for up to 5 days.

Nutrition Information:
Calories per Serving: 173; carbs: 36g; protein: 9g; fats: 6g; phosphorus: 312mg; potassium: 333mg; sodium: 146mg

Pear, Chicken and Almond Garden Salad

Serves: 4
Cooking Time: 10 minutes

Ingredients:
2 tbsps toasted slivered almonds
1 head lettuce, torn to bite sized pieces, reserving 3 large leaves
2 fresh NW pears cut into 1-inch cubes
¼ tsp ground ginger
½ tsp prepared mustard
2 tbsps reduced-calorie mayonnaise
½ cup low fat plain yogurt
¼ tsp diced celery
½ cup green pepper, sliced lengthwise
2 cups cooked boneless, skinless chicken breasts sliced into ½-inch cubes

Directions for Cooking:
1) In a bowl mix celery, green pepper and chicken.
2) Season with salt.
3) Add ginger, mustard, mayonnaise and yogurt into bowl of chicken and mix well.
4) Fold in pears and toss to mix.
5) Arrange 4 large lettuce leaves on 4 plates.
6) Evenly divide and spread torn lettuce leaves inside the large lettuce leaves.
7) Top it with ¼ of the chicken mixture, serve and enjoy.

Nutrition Information:
Calories per Serving: 142; carbs: 17g; protein: 8g; fats: 6g; phosphorus: 114 mg; potassium: 278mg; sodium: 190mg

Pasta with Parmesan Broccoli Sauce

Serves: 6
Cooking Time: 60 minutes

Ingredients:
Pepper and salt to taste
2 tbsps olive oil, divided
¼ cup grated Parmesan cheese
5 cloves garlic, smashed and chopped
6 ½ cups fresh broccoli florets, no stems
12-oz uncooked whole wheat pasta

Directions for Cooking:
1) In a large pot of boiling water, cook pasta according to manufacturer's instructions.
2) 5 minutes before pasta is done, add broccoli into pot, cover and cook until pasta is done.
3) Drain pasta and broccoli, while reserving 1 cup of liquid. Separate broccoli from pasta.
4) Return pot into high fire and heat oil.
5) Sauté garlic until lightly browned.
6) Lower fire to medium and return broccoli. Season with pepper and salt to taste.
7) Add cheese and water, mix until well combined.
8) Turn off fire and transfer broccoli mixture into blender. Puree until smooth and creamy.
9) Return to pot and turn on fire to medium and add pasta back.
10) Cook until well combined and heated through around 5 to 10 minutes.
11) Serve and enjoy.

Nutrition Information:
Calories per Serving: 222; carbs: 46g; protein: 9g; fats: 3g; phosphorus: 248mg; potassium: 351mg; sodium: 92mg

Quesadillas with Pears

Serves: 4
Cooking Time: 20 minutes

Ingredients:
2 tbsps minced onion (green, red, or yellow)
½ cup finely chopped green or red peppers
1 cup pear cubes (fresh or canned/drained)
1 cup grated cheese (try cheddar or jack)
4 medium whole wheat tortillas

Directions for Cooking:
1) On a clean cutting board, lay two tortillas. You may also use two plates depending on your preference.
2) In each tortilla, place or spread ¼ cheese then divide the onions, peppers, and pears between the two tortillas.
3) Spread the remaining cheese onto the 2 tortillas then top off with the remaining two other tortillas.
4) Medium-heat a pan then cook for 2 to 4 minutes the first quesadilla. Once the bottom begins to turn brown, gently turn it to cook the other side until it turns brown, too.
5) Slide onto plate then cook the other or second quesadilla.
6) Once all quesadillas are cooked, cut each into 4 pieces and they are ready to serve.

Nutrition Information:
Calories per Serving: 302; carbs: 33g; protein: 13g; fats: 15g; phosphorus: 296mg; potassium: 197mg; sodium: 412mg

Quinoa, Cilantro and Cranberry Salad

Serves: 6
Cooking Time: 80 minutes

Ingredients:
Pepper to taste
1/8 tsp salt
½ cup dried cranberries
½ cup minced carrots
¼ cup toasted sliced almonds
1 lime, juiced
¼ cup chopped fresh cilantro
1 ½ tsp curry powder
1 small red onion, finely chopped
¼ cup yellow bell pepper, chopped
¼ cup red bell pepper, chopped
1 cup uncooked quinoa, rinsed
1 ½ cups water

Directions for Cooking:
1) In saucepan, bring water to a boil and add quinoa. Cover and lower fire to a simmer and cook until water is fully absorbed, around 15-20 minutes.
2) Transfer quinoa into a large salad bowl and allow to cool in the ref fully.
3) After an hour of cooling in the ref, add cranberries, carrots, almonds, lime juice, cilantro, curry powder, red onion, yellow bell pepper, and red bell pepper into salad bowl. Mix well.
4) Return bowl to ref and chill for another hour before serving.

Nutrition Information:
Calories per Serving: 149; carbs: 25g; protein: 5g; fats: 3g; phosphorus: 145mg; potassium: 263mg; sodium: 63mg

Poppy Seed-Lemon Dressing on Winter Fruit Salad

Serves: 8
Cooking Time: minutes

Ingredients:
1 pear, peeled, cored and diced
1 apple, peeled cored and diced
¼ cup dried cranberries
1 cup cashews
4 oz shredded Swiss cheese
1 head Romaine lettuce, torn into bite size pieces
1 tbsp poppy seeds
2/3 cup vegetable oil
½ tsp salt
1 tsp Dijon-style prepared mustard
2 tsps diced onion
½ cup lemon juice
½ cup white sugar

Directions for Cooking:
1) In blender, process salt, mustard, onion, lemon juice, and sugar until smooth and creamy. Slowly pour in oil as blender is running. Continue blending until smooth and creamy. Add poppy seeds, blend one more time and set aside.
2) Mix well cubed pear, cubes apple, cranberries, cashews, Swiss cheese and lettuce in a large salad bowl.
3) Pour in dressing, toss well to coat.

Nutrition Information:
Calories per Serving: 334; carbs: 20g; protein: 7g; fats: 28g; phosphorus: 172mg; potassium: 409mg; sodium: 177mg

Garden salad with Strawberries

Serves: 6
Cooking Time: 10 minutes

Ingredients:
¼ cup red bell pepper, chopped
½ cup toasted pecans
1 cup sliced fresh strawberries
½ red onion, sliced
1 head romaine lettuce, torn into bite-size pieces
1 tbsp poppy seeds
1/8 cup distilled white vinegar
¼ cup white sugar
¼ cup milk
½ cup fat free creamy salad dressing

Directions for Cooking:
1) Whisk well poppy seeds, vinegar, milk, and salad dressing in a small bowl.
2) In a large salad bowl, mmix red bell pepper, pecans, strawberries, onion and lettuce.
3) Pour in dressing, toss to coat well.
4) Serve immediately.

Nutrition Information:
Calories per Serving: 140; carbs: 14g; protein: 4g; fats: 10g; phosphorus: 106mg; potassium: 402mg; sodium: 212mg

Chapter 5 Lunch Recipes

Kidney Friendly Beefy Burritos

Serves: 6
Cooking Time: 25 minutes

Ingredients:
1-pound lean ground beef
6 burrito size flour tortillas
1/4 cup onion
1/4 cup green pepper
1/4 cup low-sodium tomato puree
1/4 teaspoon black pepper
1/4 teaspoon ground cumin

Directions for Cooking:
1) Chop onion and green pepper.
2) In a medium skillet, brown ground beef for 15 minutes; drain oil on paper towels.
3) Spray skillet with non-stick cooking spray; add onion and green pepper and cook for 3 to 5 minutes, until vegetables are softened.
4) Add beef, tomato puree, black pepper and cumin to onion/pepper mixture.
5) Mix well and cook for 3 to 5 minutes on low heat.
6) Divide the beef mixture among tortillas.
7) Roll the tortilla over burrito style, making sure that both ends are folded first so mixture does not fall out.

Nutrition Information:
Calories per Serving: 305; carbs: 26g; protein: 25g; fats: 12g; phosphorus: 240mg; potassium: 331mg; sodium: 387mg

Sea Bass with Basil-Tomato Topping

Serves: 4
Cooking Time: 13 minutes

Ingredients:
1 shallot, thinly sliced
1 tablespoon olive oil
1 tbsp balsamic vinegar
1/4 cup (packed) chopped fresh basil
2 cups cherry tomatoes (about 12 ounces)
2 garlic cloves, chopped
4 6-ounce fillets sea bass or other white fish
1 tsp freshly ground pepper

Directions for Cooking:
1) Place a rack in upper third of oven and preheat broiler. Combine shallot, garlic, tomatoes, balsamic, and oil in a medium bowl, season with pepper, and toss well. Set aside.
2) Place fish in a 13x9-inch glass baking dish.
3) Scatter tomato mixture over fish and broil until fish is opaque throughout and tomatoes have started to burst, 10–13 minutes.
4) Serve with basil scattered over top.

Nutrition Information:
Calories per Serving: 245; carbs: 13g; protein: 33g; fats: 7g; phosphorus: 346mg; potassium: 570mg; sodium: 126mg

Bell Pepper 'n Garlic Medley on Sea Bass

Serves: 4
Cooking Time: 35 minutes

Ingredients:
1 Green Bell Pepper, cored and chopped
1 Red Bell Pepper, cored and chopped
1/2 lemon, juice off
2–3 cups cooked rice or pearl couscous or orzo pasta, prepared according to package (optional)
3 Shallots, chopped
4 garlic cloves, minced
4 pieces Sea Bass fillet, no skin (each piece about 6-oz in weight and 1 1/2 inches in thickness)
Private Reserve Greek extra virgin olive oil
1/2 tbsp ground coriander
1/2 tbsp garlic powder
1 tsp Aleppo pepper (or Sweet Spanish paprika)
1 tsp ground cumin
1/2 tsp black pepper

Directions for Cooking:
1) In a small bowl, combine the last 5 ingredients to make the spice mixture. Set aside.
2) In a medium-sized skillet, heat 2 tbsp olive oil over medium-high heat until hot, around 3 minutes.
3) Add the bell peppers, shallots, and garlic. Season with salt 1 tsp of the spice mixture. Cook, stirring regularly, for 5 minutes or until the peppers have softened. Turn the heat to low and leave on low heat as you prepare the fish.
4) Pat fish dry and season with the remaining spice mixture on both sides.
5) In a large cast iron skillet, heat 1/4 cup extra virgin olive oil over medium-high, around 7 minutes.
6) Add fish pieces and push down on the middle (thickest part) for 30 seconds or so. Cook fish on one side, undisturbed, until nicely browned, about 4 to 6 minutes.

7) Using a spatula, carefully turn fish over and cook on other side for 3-4 minutes until nicely browned as well. (look for browned edges before you turn it over. If parts of the fish are stuck, you should be able to carefully scrape it with the spatula and turn. But, if the fish is entirely stuck, it's not ready to be turned over. Leave it for a little bit. It should release when ready.)
8) Remove fish from heat, immediately drizzle lemon juice. Serve hot with the bell pepper medley spooned on top.
9) Enjoy!

Nutrition Information:
Calories per Serving: 343; carbs: 37g; protein: 34g; fats: 16g; phosphorus: 1273mg; potassium: 1392mg; sodium: 96mg

Mexican Baked Beans and Rice

Serves: 6
Cooking Time: 60 minutes

Ingredients:
1 cup shredded reduced fat Monterey Jack cheese
4 garlic cloves, crushed
1 tbsp cumin
1 tbsp chili powder
1 cup chopped poblano pepper
1 cup chopped red bell pepper
1 cup frozen yellow corn
1 15-oz can no-salt added black beans, drained and rinsed
2 14.5-oz cans no salt added tomatoes, diced or crushed
1 lb skinless, boneless chicken breast cut into bite sized pieces
1 ½ cups cooked brown rice

Directions for Cooking:
1) With cooking spray grease a 3-quart shallow casserole and preheat oven to 4000F.
2) Spread cooked brown rice in bottom of casserole.
3) Layer chicken on top of brown rice.
4) Mix well garlic, seasonings, peppers, corn, beans and tomatoes in a medium bowl.
5) Evenly spread bean mixture on top of chicken.
6) Sprinkle cheese on top of beans and pop into the oven.
7) Bake for 45 minutes, remove from oven and serve.

Nutrition Information:
Calories per Serving: 264; carbs: 22g; protein: 27g; fats: 9g; phosphorus: 353mg; potassium: 682mg; sodium: 280mg

Easy Baked Shepherd's Pie

Serves: 6
Cooking Time: 25 minutes

Ingredients:
Pepper to taste
½ cup shredded cheddar cheese
¾ cup reduced sodium beef broth
4 cups frozen mixed vegetables
2 tbsps flour
1 clove garlic, minced
1 medium onion, chopped
1 lb. lean ground beef
½ cup low fat milk
2 large baking potatoes, peeled and diced

Directions for Cooking:
1) In a saucepan, bring to boil potatoes with water barely covering it.
2) Once boiling, reduce fire to a simmer and cook for 15 minutes or until soft while covered.
3) Once soft, drain potatoes, transfer to a bowl and mash. Add milk and mix well.
4) Preheat oven to 375ºF.
5) In a large skillet, grease with cooking spray and sauté garlic and onions for a minute. Add ground meat and sauté until brown around 8 to 10 minutes.
6) Add flour and sauté for another minute.
7) Add broth and mixed vegetables. Sauté until bubbly, around 5 minutes.
8) Transfer mixture into an 8-inch square baking dish. Cover the top with mashed potato mixture and sprinkle cheese on top.
9) Pop into the oven and bake until bubbly around 25 minutes.
10) Serve and enjoy.

Nutrition Information:
Calories per Serving: 1639; carbs: 27g; protein: 31g; fats: 163g; phosphorus: 425mg; potassium: 896mg; sodium: 419mg

Herb-Garlic Sauce over Pan Fried Fish

Serves: 4
Cooking Time: 10 minutes

Ingredients:
1 tablespoon extra-virgin olive oil
1 tablespoon fresh oregano roughly chopped
1 tablespoon fresh parsley roughly chopped
1 tablespoon fresh thyme roughly chopped
1.5 lbs. sea bass such as barramundi
1/2 cup low sodium chicken broth
1/2 teaspoon black pepper plus more if needed
1/4 cup all-purpose flour
1/4 cup dry white wine such as sauvignon blanc
2 cloves garlic minced
3 tablespoons butter divided
juice of one lemon about 2 tablespoons
lemon wedges for serving optional

Directions for Cooking:
1) Pat the fish dry with a paper towel.
2) In a shallow dish, mix together the flour and black pepper.
3) Dredge each piece of fish in the flour mixture, coating the entire surface, and shake off any excess.
4) In a large skillet, preferably nonstick, melt 1 tablespoon of the butter over medium high heat and add the olive oil.
5) Cook the fish in the skillet for 3-4 minutes on each side, until golden brown and fully cooked. Try not to move the fish too much, especially if you are using a pan that isn't nonstick, otherwise the fish may be more likely to stick to the bottom and not get browned as nicely.
6) Remove fish from the skillet to a plate.
7) Add one more tablespoon of butter to the skillet. Once it's melted, add the minced garlic to the skillet and sauté until fragrant, about 30 seconds.
8) Add the white wine to the skillet to deglaze, stirring up any browned bits.
9) When wine has reduced by about half, add the chicken broth and bring to a simmer.

10) Turn off heat and stir in remaining 1 tablespoon butter, lemon juice, oregano, thyme, and parsley. Taste and adjust seasoning if necessary.

11) Serve sauce on top of fish.

Nutrition Information:

Calories per Serving: 403; carbs: 10g; protein: 41g; fats: 21g; phosphorus: 431mg; potassium: 628mg; sodium: 784mg

Lemony White Beans on Sea Bass

Serves: 4
Cooking Time: 20 minutes

Ingredients:
4 (6-oz.) sustainable skinless sea bass fillets
1/2 teaspoon black pepper, divided
3 tablespoons extra-virgin olive oil, divided
5 garlic cloves, sliced
2 teaspoons fresh thyme leaves
8 cherry tomatoes, quartered (about 1/2 cup)
2/3 cup unsalted chicken stock
1 (15-oz.) can unsalted cannellini beans, rinsed and drained
5 ounces fresh baby spinach
2 tablespoons fresh lemon juice

Directions for Cooking:
1) Heat a large nonstick skillet over medium-high.
2) Sprinkle fish with 1/4 teaspoon pepper.
3) Add 1 tablespoon oil to skillet; swirl to coat.
4) Add fish; cook to desired degree of doneness, about 3 minutes on each side for medium. Remove fish from pan; discard drippings. (Do not wipe skillet clean.) Lightly tent fish with foil to keep warm.
5) Heat remaining 2 tablespoons oil in skillet over medium-high.
6) Add garlic; cook, stirring often, until light golden brown, about 1 minute.
7) Stir in thyme and tomatoes; cook, stirring often, until heated through, about 1 minute.
8) Add stock and beans; bring to a simmer.
9) Add spinach in batches, and cook, tossing gently, until spinach is wilted after each addition.
10) Stir in lemon juice and remaining 1/4 teaspoon pepper.
11) Divide bean mixture among 4 shallow bowls; nestle 1 fillet into each bowl.

Nutrition Information:
Calories per Serving: 479; carbs: 26g; protein: 65g; fats: 13g; phosphorus: 716mg; potassium: 1274mg; sodium: 326mg

Beef Curry Delight

Serves: 6
Cooking Time: 2 hours

Ingredients:
2 pounds boneless beef chuck (cut into 1 ½ inch pieces)
1 cup water
1 tsp cayenne pepper
1 tsp garlic powder
1 tsp ground turmeric
1 tsp ground coriander
1 tsp ground cumin
1 ½ (2 inches) cinnamon sticks
2 whole cloves
3 whole cardamom seeds
1 tsp ginger paste
5 green Chile peppers (finely sliced)
6 cloves garlic, minced
1 onion, chopped
3 tbsps olive oil

Directions for Cooking:

1) In a skillet, heat the olive oil over medium heat then add onion.
2) Cook onion for about 5 minutes, once it has softened, reduce heat to medium low. Then for about 15 to 20 minutes, continue cooking until onion is very tender and dark brown.
3) Stir and cook the cinnamon sticks, cloves, cardamom seeds, ginger paste, green Chiles, and garlic. Cook for 3 to 5 minutes until garlic begins to brown.
4) In the onion mixture, add or mix water, cayenne pepper, garlic powder, turmeric, coriander, and cumin. Simmer until mixture has thickened and until most water has evaporated.
5) For 1 and 1 ½ hours, cook the beef chuck pieces then simmer it over medium-low heat and stir until beef is cooked and tender.
6) Once cooked, serve it with naan or pita bread.

Nutrition Information:
Calories per Serving: 287; carbs: 5g; protein: 33g; fats: 16g; phosphorus: 304mg; potassium: 524mg; sodium: 128mg

Swordfish and Citrus Salsa Delight

Serves: 6
Cooking Time: 30 minutes

Ingredients:
1 ½ pounds swordfish steaks
1 tbsp pineapple juice concentrate (thawed)
¼ tsp cayenne pepper
1 tbsp olive oil
½ cup fresh orange juice
1 tbsp chopped fresh cilantro
2 tsps white sugar
1 tbsp diced red bell pepper
3 tbsps orange juice
2 jalapeno peppers (seeded and minced)
¼ cup diced fresh mango
½ cup canned pineapple chunks (undrained)
1 orange (peeled, sectioned, and cut into bite-size)

Directions for Cooking:
1) In a bowl, make the salsa by combining and mixing well the cilantro, oranges, sugar, pineapple chunks, diced red bell pepper, minced jalapenos, mango, and 3 tablespoons orange juice. Cover the bowl and refrigerate.
2) Mix the pineapple juice concentrate, cayenne pepper, olive oil and ½ cup orange juice in a non-reactive bowl.
3) Add swordfish steaks in the bowl of pineapple juice mixture. Coat and turn well. Ensure to marinate for about 30 minutes.
4) On a gas grill, set heat to medium-high or on an outside grill with oiled rack set 6 inches from the heat source.
5) For 12 to 15 minutes in total, grill the swordfish on each side then serve with salsa.

Nutrition Information:
Calories per Serving: 204; carbs: 13g; protein: 30g; fats: 23g; phosphorus: 251mg; potassium: 486mg; sodium: 68mg

Jambalaya, A Creole Dish

Serves: 6
Cooking Time: 80 minutes

Ingredients:

¼ cup Green onions
¼ tsp cayenne
¼ tsp Thyme
½ cup celery
½ cup Green bell peppers
½ lb. shrimp, peeled and deveined
1 tbsp olive oil
2 chicken breast halves, skinless and boneless
2 cups long grain rice
2 onions, chopped
2 tbsps Worcestershire
3 tbsps garlic, minced
3 whole tomatoes, chopped
5 cups water

Directions for Cooking:
1) Bring a large saucepan, filled with 5 cups water, to a boil. Add shrimps and boil for 2 minutes. Drain shrimps, reserve liquid and transfer to a plate.
2) In same saucepan, add the reserved liquid from shrimp, 1/3 garlic, ½ of the celery, ½ of onions, all the tomatoes and the 2 chicken breasts. Bring to a boil and once boiling, lower fire to a simmer.
3) Partially cover pan and simmer for 25 minutes or until chicken is cooked and juices run clear. Remove cooked chicken and chop coarsely once cool to handle. As for the liquid, reserve and just add more water to reach 4 cups.
4) In a Dutch oven placed on medium high fire, heat oil.
5) Mix in cayenne, thyme, Worcestershire sauce, tomatoes and juice, and the reserved cooking liquid. Cook for 5 minutes while stirring constantly to break up the tomatoes.
6) Add rice and bring to a simmer, once simmering lower fire to medium low, cover and cook for 25 minutes or until water is fully absorbed by the rice.

7) Turn off fire. Mix in cooked chicken and shrimps. Cover pot and allow to stand for 5 minutes more to continue cooking.
8) To serve, transfer to serving bowls and sprinkle with parsley.

Nutrition Information:
Calories per Serving: 519; carbs: 57g; protein: 35g; fats: 14g; phosphorus: 487mg; potassium: 683mg; sodium: 466mg

Quick Thai Chicken and Vegetable Curry

Serves: 4
Cooking Time: 20 minutes

Ingredients:
1 ½ cups cauliflower florets
1 clove garlic, minced
1 cup light coconut milk
1 cup low sodium chicken broth
1 lb chicken breasts
1 medium bell pepper, julienned
1 medium onion, halved and sliced
1 tbsp fish sauce or low sodium soy sauce
1 tbsp fresh ginger, minced
1 tbsp lime juice
1 tsp light brown sugar
1 tsp red curry paste
2 cups baby spinach
2 tsp canola oil
Lime wedges

Directions for Cooking:
1) Heat oil in a skillet over medium high flame.
2) Sauté the onion and bell pepper for four minutes or until soft.
3) Add the ginger, garlic and curry paste. Mix then add the chicken. Sauté for two minutes before adding the coconut milk, broth, brown sugar and fish sauce.
4) Add the cauliflowers and reduce the heat to medium low.
5) Simmer and stir the mixture occasionally until the chicken is cooked through.
6) Add the spinach and lime juice and cook until the spinach has wilted.
7) Serve immediately with lime wedges.

Nutrition Information:
Calories per Serving: 394; carbs: 11g; protein: 29g; fats: 28g; phosphorus: 316mg; potassium: 745mg; sodium: 252mg

Lasagna Rolls in Marinara Sauce

Serves: 9
Cooking Time: 30 minutes

Ingredients:
¼ tsp crushed red pepper
¼ tsp salt
½ cup shredded mozzarella cheese
½ cups parmesan cheese, shredded
1 14-oz package tofu, cubed
1 25-oz can of low-sodium marinara sauce
1 tbsp extra virgin olive oil
12 whole wheat lasagna noodles
2 tbsp Kalamata olives, chopped
3 cloves minced garlic
3 cups spinach, chopped

Directions for Cooking:
1) Put enough water on a large pot and cook the lasagna noodles according to package instructions. Drain, rinse and set aside until ready to use.
2) In a large skillet, sauté garlic over medium heat for 20 seconds. Add the tofu and spinach and cook until the spinach wilts. Transfer this mixture in a bowl and add parmesan olives, salt, red pepper and 2/3 cup of the marinara sauce.
3) In a pan, spread a cup of marinara sauce on the bottom. To make the rolls, place noodle on a surface and spread ¼ cup of the tofu filling. Roll up and place it on the pan with the marinara sauce. Do this procedure until all lasagna noodles are rolled.
4) Place the pan over high heat and bring to a simmer. Reduce the heat to medium and let it cook for three more minutes. Sprinkle mozzarella cheese and let the cheese melt for two minutes. Serve hot.

Nutrition Information:
Calories per Serving: 600; carbs: 65g; protein: 36g; fats: 26g; phosphorus: 627mg; potassium: 914mg; sodium: 1194mg

Creamy Gorgonzola Polenta with Summer Squash Sauté

Serves: 4
Cooking Time: 50 minutes

Ingredients:
¼ cup fresh basil, chopped
½ tsp ground pepper
¾ cup cornmeal
1 14-oz cans of vegetable broth, divided
1 cup water
1 cup water
2 small yellow summer squash, sliced
2 small zucchinis, sliced
2 tbsp extra virgin olive oil
2 tbsp flour
2/3 cup crumbled Gorgonzola cheese
3 tbsp minced garlic

Directions for Cooking:
1) In a saucepan, mix 2 ½ cups of broth and 1 cup water and bring to a boil under medium high heat. Reduce the heat to low once the liquid boils and cover the saucepan.
2) Stir occasionally until the mixture becomes thick and grainy. This should take 10 or 15 minutes. Once the mixture has achieved a thick mixture, add the Gorgonzola cheese and remove from heat.
3) In a skillet, heat oil over medium high heat and add garlic. Sauté for 30 minutes and add the squash and zucchini and cook for five minutes.
4) Sprinkle the flour over the vegetables and add the remaining 1 cup of broth. Bring to a boil and reduce the heat to low. Cook for three minutes.
5) Add the basil and serve the sauté over the polenta. Serve warm.

Nutrition Information:
Calories per Serving: 284; carbs: 36g; protein: 11g; fats: 12g; phosphorus: 187mg; potassium: 333mg; sodium: 438mg

Chicken, Charred Tomato and Broccoli Salad

Serves: 6
Cooking Time: 30 minutes

Ingredients:
¼ cup lemon juice
½ tsp chili powder
1 ½ lbs. boneless chicken breast
1 ½ lbs. medium tomato
1 tsp freshly ground pepper
1 tsp salt
4 cups broccoli florets
5 tbsp extra virgin olive oil, divided to 2 and 3 tablespoons

Directions for Cooking:
1) Place the chicken in a skillet and add just enough water to cover the chicken. Bring to a simmer over high heat. Reduce the heat once the liquid boils and cook the chicken thoroughly for 12 minutes. Once cooked, shred the chicken into bite-sized pieces.
2) On a large pot, bring water to a boil and add the broccoli. Cook for 5 minutes until slightly tender. Drain and rinse the broccoli with cold water. Set aside.
3) Core the tomatoes and cut them crosswise. Discard the seeds and set the tomatoes cut-side down on paper towels. Pat them dry.
4) In a heavy skillet, heat the pan over high heat until very hot. Brush the cut sides of the tomatoes with olive oil and place them on the pan. Cook the tomatoes until the sides are charred. Set aside.
5) In the same pan, heat the remaining 3 tablespoon olive oil over medium heat. Stir the salt, chili powder and pepper and stir for 45 seconds. Pour over the lemon juice and remove the pan from the heat.
6) Plate the broccoli, shredded chicken and chili powder mixture dressing.

Nutrition Information:
Calories per Serving: 277; carbs: 6g; protein: 28g; fats: 9g; phosphorus: 292mg; potassium: 719mg; sodium: 560mg

Chicken and Sweet Potato Stir Fry

Serves: 3
Cooking Time: 40 minutes

Ingredients:
¼ tsp salt
½ cups quinoa, rinsed and drained
1 clove garlic, minced
1 cup frozen peas
1 cup water
1 jalapeno chili pepper, chopped
1 medium onion, chopped
1 medium-sized red bell pepper, chopped
1 tsp cumin, ground
1/8 tsp black pepper
12oz boneless chicken
1med sweet potatoes, cubed
3 tbsp fresh cilantro, chopped
4 tsp canola oil

Directions for Cooking:

1) Bring to a boil water and quinoa over medium heat. Simmer until the quinoa has absorbed the water.
2) In a small saucepan, put the sweet potatoes and enough water to cover the potatoes. Bring to a boil. Drain the potatoes and discard the water.
3) In a skillet, add the chicken and cook until brown. Transfer to a bowl.
4) Using the same skillet, heat 2 tablespoon of oil and sauté the onions and jalapeno pepper for one minute.
5) Add the bell pepper, cumin and garlic. Cook for three minutes until the vegetables have softened.
6) Add the peas and chicken. Cook for two minutes before adding the sweet potato and quinoa.
7) Stir cilantro and add salt and pepper to taste.
8) Serve and enjoy.

Nutrition Information:

Calories per Serving: 415; carbs: 39g; protein: 28g; fats: 18g; phosphorus: 410mg; potassium: 1201mg; sodium: 297mg

Chapter 6 Dinner Recipes

Kidney-Friendly Meatloaf Recipe

Serves: 6
Cooking Time: 50 minutes

Ingredients:
20 squares saltine-type crackers, unsalted tops
2 tablespoons onion
1-pound lean ground beef (10% fat)
1 large egg
2 tablespoons 1% low-fat milk
1/4 teaspoon black pepper
1/3 cup catsup
1 tablespoon brown sugar
1/2 teaspoon apple cider vinegar
1 teaspoon water

Directions for Cooking:
1) Preheat oven to 350°F.
2) Place crackers in a large zip-lock type plastic bag. Crush with a rolling pin.
3) Chop onion finely.
4) Coat a nonstick loaf pan lightly with cooking spray.
5) In large bowl, mix well crushed crackers, onion, ground beef, egg, milk and black pepper.
6) Place mixture in prepared pan. Cover top of pan with foil.
7) Bake for 40 minutes.
8) To make topping sauce, mix catsup, brown sugar, vinegar and water in a small bowl.
9) Remove cooked meatloaf from oven and cover with sauce.
10) Return pan to oven without the foil covering and bake for 10 additional minutes.
11) Slice into 6 portions and serve.

Nutrition Information:

Calories per Serving: 237; carbs: 13g; protein: 22g; fats: 11g; phosphorus: 177mg; potassium: 294mg; sodium: 129mg

Squash and Eggplant Casserole

Serves: 8
Cooking Time: 60 minutes

Vegetable Ingredients:
Pepper to taste
2 cups low sodium vegetable broth
½ cup dry white wine
1 red bell pepper, seeded and cut to julienned strips
1 eggplant, halved and cut to 1-inch slices
1 small butternut squash, cut into 1-inch slices
12 baby corn
1 large onion, cut into wedges
1 tbsp olive oil

Polenta Ingredients:
2 tbsp fresh oregano, chopped
¼ cup parmesan cheese, grated
1 cup instant polenta

Topping Ingredients:
5 tbsp parsley, chopped
Grated zest of 1 lemon
1 garlic clove, chopped
2 tbsp slivered almonds

Directions for Cooking:
1) Preheat the oven to 350 degrees Fahrenheit.
2) In a casserole, heat the oil and add the onion wedges and baby corn. Sauté over medium high heat for five minutes. Stir occasionally to prevent the onions and baby corn from sticking at the bottom of the pan.
3) Add the butternut squash to the casserole and toss the vegetables. Add the eggplants and the red pepper.
4) Cover the vegetables and cook over low to medium heat.
5) Cook for about ten minutes before adding the wine. Let the wine sizzle before stirring in the broth. Bring to a boil and cook in the oven for 30 minutes.

6) While the casserole is cooking inside the oven, make the topping by spreading the slivered almonds on a baking tray and toasting under the grill until they are lightly browned.
7) Place the toasted almonds in a small bowl and mix the remaining ingredients for the toppings.
8) Prepare the polenta. In a large saucepan, bring 3 cups of water to boil over high heat.
9) Add the polenta and continue whisking until it absorbs all the water.
10) Reduce the heat to medium until the polenta is thick. Add the parmesan cheese and oregano.
11) Serve the polenta on plates and add the casserole on top. Sprinkle the toppings on top.

Nutrition Information:
Calories per Serving: 126; carbs: 15g; protein: 6g; fats:5 g; phosphorus: 117mg; potassium: 618mg; sodium: 222mg

Delicious Thai Salad with Beef Strips

Serves: 6
Cooking Time: 25 minutes

Ingredients:
1 tbsp cornstarch
1 tbsp minced ginger root
1 tbsp fresh lime juice
2 cloves garlic, minced
1 tsp sesame oil
1 tsp Asian chili sauce
1 lb. Beef Strip Loin, Top Sirloin or Flank Steak, thinly sliced

Salad Ingredients:
8 cups torn romaine lettuce
4 tsp olive oil
1/2 cup halved grape tomatoes
½ cup julienned cucumber
½ cup sweet yellow pepper
½ cup red onion

Vinaigrette Ingredients:
1 tsp grated lime rind
1/4 cup fresh lime juice
2 tbsp rice vinegar
1 tbsp sodium-reduced soy sauce
1 tbsp liquid honey
1 tbsp Asian chili sauce

Directions for Cooking:
1) Combine cornstarch, ginger root, lime juice, garlic, sesame oil and chili sauce in a medium bowl.
2) Add beef and toss to coat. Let it marinate for 10 minutes. Discard marinade.
3) Heat 1 tsp olive oil in large frypan or wok over medium-high heat.
4) Stir-fry tomatoes, cucumber, yellow pepper and onion until just wilted. Transfer to a clean bowl.

5) Heat remaining oil in same pan. Stir-fry beef until browned and cooked, around 7 minutes. Add to wilted vegetables and toss to combine.
6) Whisk all vinaigrette ingredients together. Makes 1/2 cup.
7) Add Vinaigrette to pan. Cook and stir over medium heat until slightly thickened and hot, scraping up browned bits from the bottom of the pan.
8) Toss romaine with just enough hot vinaigrette to moisten.
9) Top romaine with beef and vegetable mixture. Drizzle remaining vinaigrette over each bowl.

Nutrition Information:
Calories per Serving: 184; carbs: 14g; protein: 20g; fats: 7g; phosphorus: 200mg; potassium: 548mg; sodium: 140mg

Filling Steakhouse Salad

Serves: 4
Cooking Time: 25 minutes

Ingredients:
6 medium tomatoes cut into ¼ wedges
8 cups mesclun
2 garlic cloves
2 tsp extra virgin olive oil
3 tbsp balsamic vinegar
1 lb. green beans, trimmed
½ tsp pepper
10-oz timed filet mignon
4 medium red bell peppers, seeded and halved

Directions for Cooking:
1) Preheat the grill or the broiler. Put the red peppers on the grill and cook until the skin blisters and chars. Peel away blackened skins and cut into chunks.
2) Meanwhile, lay the filet mignon on a cutting board and slit it lengthwise until it opens like a book when pressed flat. Sprinkle with ¼ teaspoon pepper. Cut 1 garlic clove and rub the cut sides all over the steak. Grill the beef until done. Slice it thinly and set aside.
3) In a sauce pan, cook the beans in the boiling water until tender. Drain and rinse with cold water. Set aside.
4) Mince the remaining garlic and add to vinegar, oil and shallot. Season with pepper.
5) In a plate, prepare a mesclun bead and arrange the steak, beans, tomatoes and red peppers on top. Drizzle with the dressing. Serve warm.

Nutrition Information:
Calories per Serving: 238; carbs: 28g; protein: 23g; fats: 6g; phosphorus: 322mg; potassium: 1514 mg; sodium: 387 mg

Stir-Fried Apples and Shrimp

Serves: 2
Cooking Time: 15 minutes

Ingredients:
1/2 lb. shrimp deveined and shelled
3/4 Apple diced
2 Celery stalks, diced
1/2 Sweet red pepper, diced
2 tbsp olive oil
1 tsp Cornstarch
Dash of White pepper

Sauce Ingredients:
1/2 tsp low sodium soy sauce
1 tsp Sugar
1 tsp cornstarch
2 tbsp cold water

Directions for Cooking:
1) Mix well cornstarch and a dash of pepper.
2) Add shrimp and marinate shrimp for 30 minutes.
3) Combine sauce ingredients in a small bowl. Mix well and set aside.
4) Heat about 1 tablespoon of oil in a non-stick wok. Stir fry shrimp until the shrimp turns pink in color, around 3 minutes on high fire. Transfer to a plate.
5) Heat remaining oil in same wok.
6) Stir fry celery briefly, and then add the diced apple and red pepper, stirring until almost cooked through, around 4 minutes on medium high fire.
7) Add the shrimp and the sauce mixture and stir constantly, for 3 minutes.
8) Once the sauce thickens it is ready to serve.

Nutrition Information:
Calories per Serving: 258; carbs: 16g; protein: 16g; fats: 15g; phosphorus: 292mg; potassium: 260mg; sodium: 184mg

Garden Salad with Oranges and Grilled Chicken

Serves: 4
Cooking Time: 10 minutes

Ingredients:
2 navel oranges, peeled and segmented
8 cups leaf lettuce, washed and dried
2 garlic cloves
4 boneless, skinless chicken breasts, 4-oz each
Cracked black pepper to taste
1 tbsp finely chopped celery
1 tbsp finely chopped red onion
1 tbsp extra virgin olive oil
4 garlic cloves, minced
½ cup red wine vinegar

Directions for Cooking:
1) Prepare the dressing by mixing pepper, celery, onion, olive oil, garlic and vinegar in a small bowl. Whisk well to combine.
2) Lightly grease grate and preheat grill to high.
3) Rub chicken with the garlic cloves and discard garlic.
4) Grill chicken for 5 minutes per side or until cooked through.
5) Remove from grill and let it stand for 5 minutes before cutting into ½-inch strips.
6) In 4 serving plates, evenly arrange two cups lettuce, ¼ of the sliced oranges and 4 olives per plate.
7) Top each plate with ¼ serving of grilled chicken, evenly drizzle with dressing, serve and enjoy.

Nutrition Information:
Calories per Serving: 101; carbs: 12g; protein: 8g; fats: 2g; phosphorus: 94mg; potassium: 298mg; sodium: 50mg

Mediterranean Style Roasted Vegetables with Polenta

Serves: 6
Cooking Time: 30 minutes

Ingredients:
2 tsps oregano
6 dry-packed sun-dried tomatoes, soaked in water to rehydrate, drained and chopped
2 plum or Roma tomatoes, sliced
10-oz frozen spinach, thawed
¼ tsp cracked black pepper
2 tsps trans-free margarine
1 ½ cups coarse polenta
6 cups water
2 tbsps + 1 tsp extra virgin olive oil
1 sweet red pepper, seeded, cored and cut into chunks
6 medium mushrooms, sliced
1 small green zucchini, cut into ¼-inch slices
1 small yellow zucchini, cut into ¼-inch slices
1 small eggplant, peeled and cut into ¼-inch slices

Directions for Cooking:
1) Grease a baking sheet and a 12-inch circle baking dish, position oven rack 4-inches away from heat source and preheat broiler.
2) With 1 tbsp olive oil, brush red pepper, mushrooms, zucchini and eggplant. Place in prepared baking sheet in a single layer. Pop in the broiler and broil under low setting.
3) Turn and brush again with oil the veggies after 5 minutes. Continue broiling until veggies are slightly browned and tender.
4) Wash and drain spinach. Set aside.
5) Preheat oven to 350°F.
6) Bring water to a boil in a medium saucepan.
7) Whisk in polenta and lower fire to a simmer. For 5 minutes, cook and stir.
8) Once polenta no longer sticks to pan, add 1/8 tsp pepper and margarine. Mix well and turn off fire.

9) Evenly spread polenta on base of prepped baking dish. Brush tops with olive oil and for ten minutes bake in the oven.
10) When done, remove polenta from oven and keep warm.
11) With paper towels remove excess water from spinach. Layer spinach on top of polenta followed by sliced tomatoes, sun-dried tomatoes, and roasted veggies. Season with remaining pepper and bake for another 10 minutes.
12) Remove from oven, cut into equal servings and enjoy.

Nutrition Information:
Calories per Serving: 129; carbs: 24g; protein: 5g; fats: 3g; phosphorus: 87mg; potassium: 600mg; sodium: 226mg

Red Curry with Vegetables

Serves: 6
Cooking Time: 30 minutes

Ingredients:
1 lime, quartered
1/3 cup cilantro, chopped
2 tsp lime juice
1 tbsp brown sugar
½ lb green beans, trimmed and cut to 1-inch pieces
2 tsp red Thai curry paste
½ cup vegetable broth or low sodium chicken broth
1 14oz can light coconut milk
1 lb sweet potatoes, cubed
1 14oz package firm tofu, cubed
4 tsp canola oil, divided

Directions for Cooking:
1) Heat 2 teaspoon of oil in a non-stick skillet over medium high heat. Sauté the tofu and cook for three minutes until brown.
2) Transfer to a plate and set aside.
3) In the same skillet, add 2 teaspoon of olive oil over medium high heat.
4) Add the sweet potatoes until browned.
5) Add the broth, coconut milk and curry paste to taste. Bring to a boil and reduce to a simmer until the sweet potatoes are tender.
6) Add the tofu, brown sugar and beans and let it simmer for two or four minutes.
7) Stir in the lime juices. Sprinkle with cilantro and serve with lime wedges.

Nutrition Information:
Calories per Serving: 355; carbs: 25g; protein: 14g; fats: 25g; phosphorus: 250mg; potassium: 747mg; sodium: 40mg

Turkey with Blueberry Pan Sauce

Serves: 4
Cooking Time: 35 minutes

Ingredients:
3 tbsp balsamic vinegar
2 cups blueberries
1 tbsp fresh thyme, chopped
¼ cup shallots, chopped
1 tbsp extra virgin olive oil
1 lb turkey tenderloin
½ tsp ground pepper
¾ tsp salt, divided
¼ cup all-purpose flour

Directions for Cooking:
1) In a shallow dish, mix together ½ tsp salt, flour and pepper. Dredge the turkey in this mixture and discard the leftover flour.
2) In an ovenproof skillet, heat oil and add the turkey. Cook for three to five minutes on each side or until golden brown.
3) Turn off the heat and transfer the skillet with the turkey in the oven. Roast it in 450 degrees Fahrenheit preheated oven for 15 minutes or until the turkey is cooked through. Remove the turkey.
4) In the same skillet, sauté the shallots and thyme for thirty seconds.
5) Add the blueberries, ¼ tsp salt and vinegar and cook for 4 to 5 minutes.
6) Plate the turkey slices with the blueberry sauce.
7) Serve warm.

Nutrition Information:
Calories per Serving: 230; carbs: 20g; protein: 29g; fats: 4g; phosphorus: 254mg; potassium: 392mg; sodium: 599mg

Chicken Soup with Kale and Sweet Potatoes

Serves: 6
Cooking Time: 60 minutes

Ingredients:
1-inch thumb sized Fresh ginger, peeled and grated
Pepper to taste
3 cups water
3 cups low-sodium chicken broth
2 tbsps apple cider vinegar
10 grape tomatoes, halved
3 cups kale, roughly chopped
1 lb sweet potatoes, peeled and chopped
3 celery stalks, chopped
4 cloves garlic, diced
1 medium-sized onion
2 ½ tbsps olive oil
1 lb skinless, boneless chicken breasts

Directions for Cooking:
1) With pepper, season chicken to taste.
2) On medium high fire, place soup pot and add oil.
3) Pan fry chicken until golden brown, around 4 minutes per side. Remove chicken from pot and put aside for the meantime.
4) In same pot, add onion, garlic and celery. Sauté for 7-8 minutes or until tender.
5) Pour vinegar and sauté for a minute.
6) Add water, chicken broth, tomatoes, kale, and sweet potatoes and bring to a boil. Once boiling, slow fire to a simmer and cook for 20 minutes.
7) While waiting, tear chicken for a pulled effect, with hands.
8) Fifteen minutes into simmering time, add chicken to soup to heat through.
9) To serve, spoon soup into bowls and top with freshly grated ginger.

Nutrition Information:
Calories per Serving: 272; carbs: 20g; protein: 28g; fats: 10g; phosphorus: 280mg; potassium: 884mg; sodium: 429mg

Parsnip and Pear Soup

Serves: 4
Cooking Time: 35 minutes

Ingredients:
1 tbsp olive oil
Pepper to taste
½ tsp rosemary
1 tsp thyme
1 tsp sage
1 clove garlic crushed
1 bay leaf
2 pears, peeled and chopped
2-3 cups vegetable stock
2 parsnips, peeled and chopped
2 cups cauliflower florets
½ leek, washed and sliced
1 tbsp chives

Directions for Cooking:
1) On medium fire, place a soup pot and heat oil.
2) Once oil is hot, sauté leeks for 5 minutes.
3) Add stock, bay leaf, herbs, pear, garlic, parsnips and cauliflower. Bring to a simmer and slow fire to medium low and continue cooking for 25 minutes.
4) With an immersion blender, puree soup until smooth.
5) Add pepper to taste.
6) Serve topped with chives

Nutrition Information:
Calories per Serving: 198; carbs: 35g; protein: 6g; fats: 6g; phosphorus: 146mg; potassium: 856mg; sodium: 381mg

Chickpeas Soup Moroccan Style

Serves: 4
Cooking Time: 40 minutes

Ingredients:
2 handfuls baby spinach
1 tbsp tomato paste, no added salt
¼ tsp ground coriander
¼ tsp cumin
¼ tsp paprika, smoked or sweet
1 carrot, diced
¼ tsp chili
1 can chickpeas, drained and rinsed
1 clove garlic
½ lemon juiced and zested
1 large tomato, diced
1 cup water
2 cups stock
2 celery sticks, sliced
1 onion, diced
1 tbsp olive oil

Directions for Cooking:
1) On medium high fire, place a soup pot and heat oil.
2) Add onions and sauté for 3 minutes.
3) Add carrot, chili and celery. For 3 minutes more, continue sautéing.
4) Add garlic, paprika, coriander, and cumin. Cook for a minute.
5) Add chickpeas, lemon juice and zest, tomato, water and stock. Bring to a boil and once simmering slow fire to low.
6) While covered, simmer soup for 20 minutes.
7) Add tomato paste and baby spinach. Continue simmering for another ten minutes.
8) Ladle soup to serving bowls and best enjoyed with a side of crusty bread.

Nutrition Information:
Calories per Serving: 169; carbs: 22g; protein: 10g; fats: 6g; phosphorus: 209mg; potassium: 1039mg; sodium: 282mg

Swiss Chard, White Bean & Pasta Soup

Serves: 6
Cooking Time: 20 minutes

Ingredients:
¾ cup fine egg noodles, cooked and drained
1 cup chopped canned tomatoes
1 cup dried Great Northern beans or cannellini beans
1 small bunch red Swiss chard, thick stems removed, leaves cut into thin julienne strips
1 tbsp olive oil
2 medium carrots, peeled and coarsely chopped
2 medium yellow onions, coarsely chopped
3 garlic cloves, minced
3 tbsps finely chopped fresh basil
4 tbsps finely chopped fresh flat leaf parsley
6 cups chicken broth
6 tbsps Grated Parmigiano-Reggiano Cheese
Pepper and salt to taste

Directions for Cooking:
1) The night before, pick and discard any misshapen beans. Then soak while fully covered in water overnight. The next day, drain and discard water from beans.
2) On medium high fire, place a soup pot and heat oil.
3) Add onions and sauté for 5 minutes or until soft.
4) Add carrots, for 3 minutes, sauté it.
5) Add half of Swiss chard and sauté for 3 minutes or until wilted.
6) Add garlic, basil, tomatoes, beans and broth. Simmer for an hour until beans are soft while partially covered.
7) Turn off fire and with an immersion blender, puree soup until smooth.
8) Turn on fire to medium high and add remaining chard and pasta.
9) Cook for 3 minutes. Season to taste with pepper and salt.
10) Add 2 tbsps parsley, mix well and turn off fire.
11) To serve, ladle soup equally into serving bowls, garnish with remaining parsley and cheese.

Nutrition Information:
Calories per Serving: 231; carbs: 30g; protein: 13g; fats: 7.3g; phosphorus: 208mg; potassium: 741mg; sodium: 526mg

Stir-Fried Mango-Chicken with Broccoli

Serves: 6
Cooking Time: 15 minutes

Ingredients:
¼ cup chopped fresh basil
¼ cup chopped fresh cilantro
¼ cup chopped fresh mint
¼ cup water
1 bunch scallions, cut into 1-inch length
1 fresh small red or green chile peppers, stemmed and sliced
1 lime cut into 6 wedges, for garnish
1 teaspoon minced fresh ginger
1-pound chicken tenders, cut into 1-inch pieces
2 cloves garlic, minced
2 mangoes, peeled and sliced
2 tablespoons + 1 teaspoon fish sauce
2 tablespoons lime juice
4 cups bit sized broccoli florets
4 teaspoons olive oil, divided

Directions for Cooking:
1) In a small bowl, mix cornstarch, lime juice and fish sauce.
2) On high fire, heat 2 teaspoons oil in a large skillet. Sauté chicken for 5-7 minutes or until cooked through. When done, put on a plate.
3) In same pan, heat remaining oil. Sauté chiles, ginger, and garlic for a minute or until fragrant. Add water and broccoli and sauté for two minutes or until broccoli start to soften. Add scallions and mangoes, stir fry for a minute. Add chicken and fish sauce mixture. Stirring constantly, continue sautéing until chicken is heated through and sauce has thickened. Stir in mint, basil and cilantro and turn off fire. Mix well before transferring to a serving platter.
4) To serve, garnish with lemon wedges.

Nutrition Information:
Calories per Serving: 211; carbs: 15g; protein: 24g; fats: 7g; phosphorus: 177mg; potassium: 491mg; sodium: 229mg

Chapter 7 Snack Recipes

Scrumptious Apple Bars

Serves: 18
Cooking Time: 35 minutes

Ingredients:
1 cup granulated sugar
1 cup powdered sugar
1 cup sour cream
1 teaspoon baking soda
1 teaspoon cinnamon
1 teaspoon vanilla extract
1/2 cup brown sugar
1/2 teaspoon salt
2 cups all-purpose flour
2 medium apples
2 tablespoons milk
3/4 cup unsalted butter

Directions for Cooking:
1) Preheat the oven to 350°F.
2) Peel and chop the apples.
3) Cream 1/2 cup of butter and granulated sugar.
4) Add sour cream, vanilla, baking soda, salt and flour. Mix well.
5) Stir in chopped apples.
6) Pour batter into a greased 9 x 13-inch baking pan.
7) In a small bowl, mix 2 tablespoons of softened butter, the brown sugar and cinnamon together. Sprinkle over top of the batter.
8) Bake for 35 minutes.
9) Let cool completely.
10) To make icing, combine 2 tablespoons melted butter, milk (or milk substitute) and powdered sugar.
11) Drizzle over top and cut dessert into 18 bars.

Nutrition Information:

Calories per Serving: 181; carbs: 29g; protein: 2.3g; fats: 6.72g; phosphorus: 31mg; potassium: 74mg; sodium: 80mg

Deliciously Good Tuna Dip

Serves: 4
Cooking Time: 0 minutes

Ingredients:
1 can (170 g) no salt added tuna in water, drained
1 tsp lemon juice
1/2 tsp Dijon mustard
2 Tbsp light mayonnaise
pepper to taste

Directions for Cooking:
1) Place tuna in a bowl and shred.
2) Add remaining ingredients and mix well.
3) Best served with your low salt cracker or sourdough bread.

Nutrition Information:
Calories per Serving: 80; carbs: 2g; protein: 12g; fats: 4g; phosphorus: 76mg; potassium: 140mg; sodium: 86mg

Almond Walnut Granola

Serves: 24
Cooking Time: 30 minutes

Ingredients:
¼ cup canola oil
½ cup unsweetened coconut, shredded
¾ cups walnuts, chopped
1 ½ tsp vanilla
1 cup almonds, slivered
1 cup raisins
2 cups bran flakes
4 tbsp honey
6 cups rolled oats (old fashioned)

Directions for Cooking:
1) Prepare a baking sheet by lightly spraying with cooking spray and preheat oven to 325°F.
2) On low fire, place a small saucepan and add vanilla, honey and oil. Cook for 5 minutes while stirring occasionally to combine thoroughly.
3) In a large mixing bowl, thoroughly combine walnuts, bran flakes, coconut, almonds, and oats.
4) Pour in the honey mixture while mixing to coat ingredients evenly.
5) Spread mixture in an even layer on baking tray, pop in the oven and bake until lightly browned and crisped. This will take around 25 minutes of baking.
6) Remove from oven and cool. Once cooled, mix in raisins. One serving is equal to a half cup.

Nutrition Information:
Calories per Serving: 154; carbs: 23g; protein: 6g; fats: 9g; phosphorus: 228mg; potassium: 206mg; sodium: 33mg

Pumpkin Walnut Cookie

Serves: 48
Cooking Time: 15 minutes

Ingredients:
½ cup olive oil
1 ½ cups brown sugar
1 ¾ cups pumpkin, cooked and pureed (15 oz. can)
1 cup raisin
1 cup walnuts or hazelnuts, chopped
1 tbsp baking powder
1¼ cups whole wheat flour
1½ cups flour
1½ tsp pumpkin pie spice mix
2 eggs

Directions for Cooking:
1) Grease a cookie sheet with cooking spray and preheat oven to 400°F.
2) In a medium bowl mix baking powder, salt, pumpkin pie spice mix, whole wheat flour and flour.
3) In a large bowl beat eggs and oil thoroughly.
4) Add in brown sugar and beat for at least 3 minutes.
5) Mix in pumpkin puree and beat well.
6) Slowly add the dry ingredients beating well after each addition.
7) Fold in nuts and raisins.
8) Using a 1 tbsp measuring spoon, get a tablespoon full of the dough and place on cookie sheet at least 2-inches apart. With the bottom of a spoon, flatten cookie.
9) Pop into the oven and bake until golden brown, around 10-12 minutes.
10) Once done, remove from oven, serve and enjoy or store in tightly lidded containers for up to a week.

Nutrition Information:
Calories per Serving: 113; carbs: 15g; protein: 3g; fats: 5g; phosphorus: 71mg; potassium: 125mg; sodium: 17mg

Choco-Chip Cookies with Walnuts and Oatmeal

Serves: 48
Cooking Time: 32 minutes

Ingredients:
½ cup all-purpose flour
½ cup chopped walnuts
½ cup whole wheat pastry flour
½ tsp baking soda
1 cup semisweet Choco chip
1 large egg
1 large egg white
1 tbsp vanilla extract
1 tsp ground cinnamon
2 cups rolled oats (not quick-cooking)
2/3 cup granulated sugar
2/3 cup packed light brown sugar
4 tbsps cold unsalted butter, cut into pieces

Directions for Cooking:
1) Position two racks in the middle of the oven, leaving at least a 3-inch space in between them. Preheat oven to 350°F and grease baking sheets with cooking spray.
2) In medium bowl, whisk togetherbaking soda, cinnamon, whole wheat flour, all-purpose flour and oats.
3) In a large bowl, with a mixer beat butter until well combined.
4) Add brown sugar and granulated sugar, mixing continuously until creamy.
5) Mix in vanilla, egg white and egg and beat for a minute.
6) Cup by cup mix in the dry ingredients until well incorporated.
7) Fold in walnuts and Choco chips.
8) Get a tablespoon full of the batter and roll with your moistened hands into a ball.
9) Evenly place balls into prepped baking sheets at least 2-inches apart.
10) Pop in the oven and bake for 16 minutes. Ten minutes into baking time, switch pans from top to bottom and bottom to top. Continue baking for 6 more minutes.

11) Remove from oven, cool on a wire rack. Allow pans to cool completely before adding the next batch of cookies to be baked.
12) Cookies can be stored for up to 2-weeks in a tightly sealed container or longer in the ref.

Nutrition Information:
Calories per Serving: 71; carbs: 12g; protein: 2g; fats: 3g; phosphorus: 47mg; potassium: 56mg; sodium: 18mg

Walnut Butter on Cracker

Serves: 1
Cooking Time: 0 minutes

Ingredients:
1 tablespoon walnut butter
2 pieces Mary's gone crackers

Directions for Cooking:
1) Spread ½ tablespoon of walnut butter per cracker and enjoy.

Nutrition Information:
Calories per Serving: 134; carbs: 4g; protein: 1g; fats: 14g; phosphorus: 19mg; potassium: 11mg; sodium: 138mg

Roasted Bananas with Chocolate Yogurt Cream

Serves: 4
Cooking Time: 5 minutes

Ingredients:
½ cup whipping cream
½ tsp ground cinnamon
1 ½ cups low fat vanilla yogurt, chilled and drained
1 tbsp cold butter
1 tbsp confectioner's sugar
1 tbsp dark rum or lemon juice
2 tbsp unsweetened cocoa powder
3 tbsp dark brown sugar
4 bananas cut in strips

Directions for Cooking:
1) Place bananas cut side up on a baking sheet coated with cooking spray.
2) Sprinkle with brown sugar, rum and cinnamon. Dot with butter.
3) Roast in a 425-degree Fahrenheit preheated oven for five minutes. Turn the broiler off until the bananas are golden.
4) Meanwhile, beat the cocoa, cream and confectioner's sugar in a large bowl using an electric mixer.
5) Add the drained yogurt and fold the cream until well combined.
6) Plate the roasted bananas and add a dollop of chocolate cream on top.

Nutrition Information:
Calories per Serving: 236; carbs: 42g; protein: 7g; fats: 7g; phosphorus: 186mg; potassium: 727mg; sodium: 91mg

Pineapple Raspberry Parfaits

Serves: 2
Cooking Time: 0 minutes

Ingredients:
½ pint fresh raspberries
1 ½ cup fresh or frozen pineapple chunks
2 8oz containers non-fat peach yogurt

Directions for Cooking:
1) In a parfait glass, layer the yogurt, raspberries and pineapples alternately.
2) Chill inside the refrigerator.
3) Serve chilled.

Nutrition Information:
Calories per Serving: 319; carbs: 60g; protein: 22g; fats: 1g; phosphorus: 293mg; potassium: 479mg; sodium: 85mg

Chapter 8 Dessert Recipes

Grilled Peach Sundaes

Serves: 1
Cooking Time: 5 minutes

Ingredients:
1 tbsp toasted unsweetened coconut
1 tsp canola oil
2 peaches, halved and pitted
2 scoops non-fat vanilla yogurt, frozen

Directions for Cooking:
1) Brush the peaches with oil and grill until tender.
2) Place peach halves on a bowl and top with frozen yogurt and coconut.

Nutrition Information:
Calories per Serving: 61; carbs: 2g; protein: 2g; fats: 6g; phosphorus: 32mg; potassium: 85mg; sodium: 30mg

Blueberry Swirl Cake

Serves: 9
Cooking Time: 45 minutes

Ingredients:
½ cup margarine
1 ¼ cups reduced fat milk
1 cup granulated sugar
1 egg
1 egg white
1 tbsp lemon zest, grated
1 tsp cinnamon
1/3 cup light brown sugar
2 ½ cups fresh blueberries
2 ½ cups self-rising flour

Directions for Cooking:
1) Cream the margarine and granulated sugar using an electric mixer at high speed until fluffy.
2) Add the egg and egg white and beat for another two minutes.
3) Add the lemon zest and reduce the speed to low.
4) Add the flour with milk alternately.
5) In a greased 13x19 pan, spread half of the batter and sprinkle with blueberry on top. Add the remaining batter.
6) Bake in a 350-degree Fahrenheit preheated oven for 45 minutes.
7) Let it cool on a wire rack before slicing and serving.

Nutrition Information:
Calories per Serving: 384; carbs: 63g; protein: 7g; fats: 13g; phosphorus: 264mg; potassium: 158mg; sodium: 456mg

Peanut Butter Cookies

Serves: 24
Cooking Time: 24 minutes

Ingredients:
¼ cup granulated sugar
1 cup unsalted peanut butter
1 tsp baking soda
2 cups all-purpose flour
2 large eggs
2 tbsp butter
2 tsp pure vanilla extract
4 ounces softened cream cheese

Directions for Cooking:
1) Line a cookie sheet with a non-stick liner. Set aside.
2) In a bowl, mix flour, sugar and baking soda. Set aside.
3) On a mixing bowl, combine the butter, cream cheese and peanut butter.
4) Mix on high speed until it forms a smooth consistency. Add the eggs and vanilla gradually while mixing until it forms a smooth consistency.
5) Add the almond flour mixture slowly and mix until well combined.
6) The dough is ready once it starts to stick together into a ball.
7) Scoop the dough using a 1 tablespoon cookie scoop and drop each cookie on the prepared cookie sheet.
8) Press the cookie with a fork and bake for 10 to 12 minutes at 350°F.

Nutrition Information:
Calories per Serving: 138; carbs: 12g; protein: 4g; fats: 9g; phosphorus: 60mg; potassium: 84mg; sodium: 31mg

Banana Foster Pie

Serves: 8
Cooking Time: 0 minutes

Ingredients:
½ cup coconut sugar
½ cup melted coconut oil
½ teaspoon nutmeg
¾ cup cashew butter
1 9-inch prepared pie crust
1 tablespoon coconut oil
1/3 cup arrowroot starch
2 ¼ teaspoon dark rum
2 teaspoon cinnamon
2 teaspoon vanilla extract
3 cups coconut cream
4 ripe bananas, sliced

Directions for Cooking:
1) In a bowl, whip the coconut cream until fluffy. Add the arrowroot starch and whip for another minute. Add the cashew butter at a time. Mix in the coconut sugar, nutmeg, and cinnamon and whip for 2 more minutes until the sugar dissolves. Add the ½ cup melted coconut oil, vanilla and2 teaspoon rum. Chill the mixture for at least 30 minutes.
2) Make the caramelized banana layer by frying the bananas in 1 tablespoon of oil. Add sugar until the bananas brown. Mix in the ¼ teaspoon rum last. Reduce the heat to low and let it simmer for five minutes.
3) Assemble the pie by layering the bananas on the bottom of the prepared pie crust. Add the chilled cream.
4) Refrigerate for 6 hours.
5) Garnish with more coconut sugar on top.

Nutrition Information:
Calories per Serving: 598; carbs: 40g; protein: 7g; fats: 49g; phosphorus: 156mg; potassium: 402mg; sodium: 234mg

Deliciously Good Scones

Serves: 10
Cooking Time: 12 minutes

Ingredients:
¼ cup dried apricots, chopped
¼ cup dried cranberries
¼ cup sunflower seeds
½ teaspoon baking soda
1 large egg
2 cups all-purpose flour
2 tablespoon honey

Directions for Cooking:
1) Preheat the oven to 350°F.
2) Grease a baking sheet. Set aside.
3) In a bowl, mix the salt, baking soda and flour. Add the dried fruits, nuts and seeds. Set aside.
4) In another bowl, mix the honey and eggs.
5) Add the wet ingredients to the dry ingredients. Use your hands to mix the dough.
6) Create 10 small round doughs and place them on the baking sheet.
7) Bake for 12 minutes.

Nutrition Information:
Calories per Serving: 44; carbs: 27g; protein: 4g; fats: 3g; phosphorus: 59mg; potassium: 92mg; sodium: 65mg

Mixed Berry Cobbler

Serves: 8
Cooking Time: 4 hours

Ingredients:
¼ cup coconut milk
¼ cup ghee
¼ cup honey
½ cup almond flour
½ cup tapioca starch
½ tablespoon cinnamon
½ tablespoon coconut sugar
1 teaspoon vanilla
12 ounces frozen raspberries
16 ounces frozen wild blueberries
2 teaspoon baking powder
2 teaspoon tapioca starch

Directions for Cooking:
1) Place the frozen berries in the slow cooker. Add honey and 2 teaspoons of tapioca starch. Mix to combine.
2) In a bowl, mix the tapioca starch, almond flour, coconut milk, ghee, baking powder and vanilla. Sweeten with sugar. Place this pastry mix on top of the berries.
3) Set the slow cooker for 4 hours.

Nutrition Information:
Calories per Serving: 146; carbs: 33g; protein: 1g; fats: 3g; phosphorus: 29mg; potassium: 133mg; sodium: 4mg

Blueberry Espresso Brownies

Serves: 12
Cooking Time: 30 minutes

Ingredients:
¼ cup organic cocoa powder
¼ teaspoon salt
½ cup raw honey
½ teaspoon baking soda
1 cup blueberries
1 cup coconut cream
1 tablespoon cinnamon
1 tablespoon ground coffee
2 teaspoon vanilla extract
3 eggs

Directions for Cooking:
1) Preheat the oven to 325°F.
2) In a bow mix together coconut cream, honey, eggs, cinnamon, honey, vanilla, baking soda, coffee and salt.
3) Use a mixer to combine all ingredients.
4) Fold in the blueberries
5) Pour the batter in a greased baking dish and bake for 30 minutes or until a toothpick inserted in the middle comes out clean.
6) Remove from the oven and let it cool.

Nutrition Information:
Calories per Serving: 168; carbs: 20g; protein: 4g; fats: 10g; phosphorus: 79mg; potassium: 169mg; sodium: 129mg

Printed in Great Britain
by Amazon